THE KEY IS THE STRATEGY

THE KEY IS THE STRATEGY

A GUIDE FOR ENTREPRENEURS

CARLOS R. MIRELES TREMOLS

THE KEY IS THE STRATEGY

A guide for entrepreneurs

Carlos Mireles Tremols

All Rights Reserved 2019 ©

It is strictly prohibited without written authorization from the copyright holder, under the established sanctions by law, the total or partial reproduction of this work by any means or procedure, as well as the distribution of unauthorized copies.

ISBN: 979-8324-36-456-4

Printed and made in Santo Domingo, Dominican Republic

Contents

PROLOGUE..11

INTRODUCTION...13

CHAPTER I: PRINCIPLES OF ECONOMICS.....................17
   1.1 Demand 19
   1.2   Supply 26
   1.3   Production Possibilities Frontier........................... 31
   1.4   Costs, Revenues, and Benefits........................... 34
      1.4.1 Business Costs 34
      1.4.2 Revenue Generation 41

CHAPTER II: ACCOUNTING..45
   2.1 Basic Items of Financial Statements 48
      2.1.1 Definitions and Basic Concepts.......................... 48
      2.1.2 Current Assets 50
      2.1.3 Fixed Assets.. 56
      2.1.4 Liabilities and Capital 57
   2.2. Balance Sheet.. 58
   2.3. Financial Ratios from the Balance Sheet................ 60
      2.3.1 Liquidity Ratios.. 60
      2.3.2 Leverage Ratios 62
   2.4. Income Statement 63
      2.4.1 Profitability Ratios.. 64
      2.4.2 Operational Ratios... 65
   2.5. Cash Flow... 67

CHAPTER III: STRATEGIC PLAN AND EXECUTION..........71

- 3.1 What is Strategy? 74
- 3.2 Creating a Strategic Plan....................................... 76
- 3.3 Market and Company Analysis 79
  - 3.3.1 Porter's Five Forces 88
- 3.4 Internal Company Analysis 94
- 3.5 Company Diagnosis 96

CHAPTER IV: OPERATIONAL PLAN AND IMPLEMENTATION...97

- 4.1 Canvas Model 105
  - 4.1.1 Key Partners 106
  - 4.1.2 Key Activities... 106
  - 4.1.3 Key Resources... 107
  - 4.1.4 Market Segment or Customers 107
  - 4.1.5 Customer Relationships 110
  - 4.1.6 Communication Channels 111
  - 4.1.7 Cost Structure 111
  - 4.1.8 Revenue Streams 112
  - 4.1.9 Value Proposition.. 112

CHAPTER V: BUSINESS IDEA REVIEW.........................115

- 5.1 Feasibility of the Business Idea............................. 120

CHAPTER VI: EXECUTION OF THE BUSINESS IDEA.......121

- 6.1 Integration with Personnel and the Business 127
- 6.2 Setting Realistic Goals and Prioritizing Objectives . 129
- 6.3 Goal Monitoring 131
- 6.4 Creating a Rewards Scheme 132
- 6.5 Employee Training.. 133

6.6 Leveraging Capabilities 133

CHAPTER VII: BUILD A LEADER FOR EXECUTION……….135

FINAL WORDS……………………………………………………..141

PROLOGUE

As an executive in the financial sector, like Carlos Mireles, who presents us with this didactic work, I am pleased to introduce this piece that brings the population closer to understanding the necessary tools for entrepreneurship.

Among the reasons that highlight the value of this noble work is its simple and precise contribution to the topics that ensure the longevity of companies, fostering an understanding of both economic and strategic definitions of great value and easy implementation, as well as essential recommendations to guide the company.

The author elaborates, with utmost rigor, a pedagogical proposal for entrepreneurship and the successful performance of businesses. While it is based on his own experiences and confirmed by the revelations of entrepreneurs in the final chapter, it is logically supported by the fields of the respective business management disciplines, making it a brilliant example of sustainability. Furthermore, it establishes the connections with various cross-cutting axes. In summary, it demonstrates complete alignment with survival parameters and good business performance.

The initial chapters present the theoretical and justifying framework for the recommendations to be found. This is the core foundation, clear and impeccable, where the economic and macro perspective is demonstrated with total precision and validation through its practical application. The final chapters constitute the materialization of the developed proposal, in which specific differentiated actions are defined alongside recommendations and testimonies to guide the journey toward a profitable and sustainable venture. The path to entrepreneurship is rocky, but by embarking on it with this book, readers can transform their vision through the lessons they will find.

The success of what you undertake depends on your preparation, relying on valuable tools and advice like those provided by Carlos in this work. I reflect on what Richard Branson recommends: "What's my biggest motivation? To keep challenging myself. I see life as one long university education that I never had. Every day, I'm learning something new."

We live in a world full of obstacles and limitations, guided by many options but with limited time and resources. Our response to these barriers is one of the most essential tasks in our businesses. This book allows you to draw from the lessons of successful companies and guide yourself with methods that challenge your goals.

Linda Valette
Break it Project – Founder
CECAFI Centro de capacitación financiera y de negocios - Founder
Member Board of Directors – PARVAL Puesto de Bolsa
First female CEO of an International Multiple Bank in the Dominican Republic

INTRODUCTION

Sometimes, why do some companies survive while others die within a year? Why do executives avoid making strategic decisions? And what causes some corporations to thrive over time while others seem to have a limited lifespan? These and other questions remain relevant even within established organizations.

Many of the difficulties companies face stem from their inability to make the right choices when developing a business idea. This, combined with the rapid pace of technological advancements, the entry of new competitors, and changes in consumer needs, makes it essential to carefully analyze what a company needs to be successful, regardless of its size or target market.

Many companies need to pay more attention to the factors that affect the execution of their operations. Furthermore, the decision-maker often needs more vision. Ultimately, it is a strategic deficiency.

A familiar mistake companies make when they realize their market position has weakened is to seek operational efficiency, as it improves their operations. They mistakenly get caught up in the process, ignoring the fact that other participants can also strengthen their activities similarly. In other words, if the focus is solely on improving the business's operations, competitors who are more open to technology, have better-trained staff, and more significant resources can apply the strategy more effectively than a participant with fewer resources. In the end, the companies will return to their initial position when, in reality, the focus should have been on doing something different from what others are doing.

Ideally, when losing market position, executives should develop a business idea or strategy that gives them a competitive advantage and sets them apart from others. It is suggested that this be based on meeting consumer needs, which means it must either be an activity not exploited by other competitors or be a similar activity to what competitors already offer but delivered to the public in a different way. In other words, the new business idea should allow these companies to have a differentiated market position.

From this perspective, the purpose of this book is to provide the necessary tools for the reader to develop a business idea with a competitive advantage that allows them to differentiate themselves from other market participants, taking into account the factors that can affect the development or enhancement of the business.

Each step of the business idea evolution process, including basic economic concepts, is examined to understand how markets interact with consumers. Accounting concepts are also presented to decipher how a company's cash conversion cycle works to maintain its operations and everything related to creating a business idea.

The material provides indispensable tools for entrepreneurs to develop a business strategy and accurately identify consumer needs. It is worth mentioning that this content applies to both new ideas and existing businesses, allowing them to grow and have the necessary inputs for innovation and a change in their strategic position in the market.

The book's distribution guides the reader first to appreciate how markets function, how companies interact with consumers, and how the company's internal financial structure is analyzed to acquire working capital and maintain healthy economic conditions. Subsequently, we move on to the strategic plan, focusing on business strategy, market analysis, internal company analysis, and company diagnosis. We then concentrate on the operational plan and its implementation, plan review, and the execution of the business idea.

Additionally, the book includes all the necessary steps and flowcharts for bringing the business idea into production, including essential aspects for the key executive to lead the new business idea. Finally, we include a compilation of recommendations from entrepreneurs in various sectors who have achieved success and longevity for their companies. They share the activities or strategies they have implemented to have a unique and prosperous business in their respective markets.

CHAPTER I: PRINCIPLES OF ECONOMICS

Before starting a business, it is essential for entrepreneurs to have a foundation of economic principles to recognize certain variables that influence the financial sector they are involved in. If they do not understand these factors, their company may not achieve the growth or reach they expect. For this reason, we begin our business model by analyzing the factors that influence the economy. The starting point is understanding supply and demand.

1.1 Demand

We have decided to start with demand because if we know what people want, what motivates them to consume, how they behave towards one sound or another, and what they are willing to sacrifice (and what they are not), we will have a market niche in which to start our business.

Irvin Tucker, author of the book "Fundamentals of Economics[1]," tells us that economics has the **Law of Demand**, which states an inverse relationship between price and quantity demanded if all other variables remain constant. This means that the higher the price of an asset, the less amount of that asset will be required compared to if the price of the asset were to decrease. This is because consumers will be less willing to spend more on as asset or service priced unreasonably. This tells us that offering low prices is the best condition for increasing the quantity of assets demanded.

Therefore, if we graph the demand curve, we will notice that it has a negative slope (higher price, lower demand), as shown in the following graph:

---

[1] Tucker I.B. (2001). Fundamentals of Economics, 3rd Ed. United States: Thomson Lerning

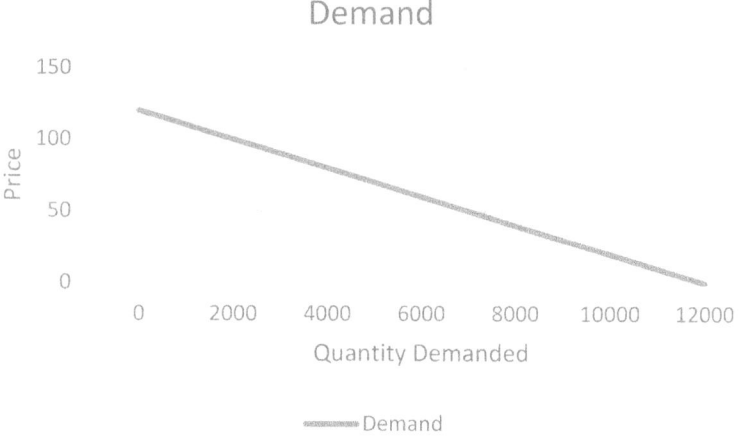

Now, we recommend considering the other factors that affect demand because understanding them allows us to comprehend why people make certain decisions. These factors include:

- ✓ Income levels.
- ✓ Market size.
- ✓ Prices and availability of related assets.
- ✓ Individual tastes or preferences.
- ✓ Buyers' expectations.
- ✓ Only when these factors remain constant can the theory explained above be applied.

It is crucial to know these elements depending on the asset or service we will market. For example, if a product or service is targeted towards a marginalized area of the country, knowing that the income level of the residents in that area will limit the quantity demanded of the asset, an increase in the wages of the target audience will increase the amount required of the product or service. Furthermore, suppose that the market size where we compete is relatively tiny or growing. In that case, the demand will be highly competitive or limited. All participants will want to capture a large portion of the market.

On the other hand, prices and availability of related products (substitutes) also affect the decisions of the target audience. This can be explained as follows: if the price of the product or service being offered is slightly higher than the value of related products (taking into consideration all the variables that affect the purchase decision), customers will choose to buy a substitute product or service instead of preferring the one we are offering.

Individual tastes or preferences are what we know as "trends" or "fads." It is helpful to know these factors because if we enter a market where the trend is fading, we may make an investment that we cannot recover, or in the short term, we may experience an economic imbalance due to the shift of consumers to another market.

Likewise, the expectations of buyers must be taken into account. It is similar to when we were young and visited the playgrounds in public parks. We played in that vast place surrounded by many children, but as we grew up, we realized the park was just a few square meters. The same thing happens to buyers, who sometimes have high expectations about the product or service they will buy due to the promotion and advertising we do. However, when they consume it, they realize that it.

This teaches us not to exaggerate the virtues and benefits of what we offer but rather to accurately indicate what the product or service is about so that we can meet or exceed the public's expectations and gain regular customers.

Another point to consider regarding buyer expectations is their future appreciation of the demand for a product or service. For example, suppose people know gasoline prices will decrease by five pesos next Friday. In that case, the demand for this product will decrease until then because it is more reasonable to wait and buy gasoline on Friday. Similarly, if a natural phenomenon such as a hurricane is forecasted to hit the country in a week, all the necessary provisions to survive this event will be consumed massively. In other words, the quantity demanded of a product or service can be affected depending on future speculations.

As we can observe, if we know that due to regulation, the price of a product or service will decrease, which means that people will only consume it once this happens, we must also reduce the quantity offered. Similarly, due to specific needs, demand will tend to increase. In that case, we can modify the price of the asset and increase production to maximize profits.

Depending on the movement of the demand curve, it has one of these three behaviors: elastic demand, unitary demand, or inelastic demand[2].

- **Elastic demand:** is when the variation between price and quantity demanded is greater than 1, meaning that in response to a price increase, the amount required will decrease proportionally more than 1.
- **Unitary demand**: as the price decreases, the demand increases in the same proportion. For example, if the price drops by 2%, the demand increases by 2%.
- **Inelastic demand**: the proportion of the price variation to the quantity demanded variation is less than 1, meaning that a 5% price increase causes the movement of the amount required to be less than 1%.

The elasticity of demand determines what type of assets or services we offer in the market. For this reason, it is essential to know the demand for each and how the curve moves in response to a change in price, assuming other variables remain constant.

The assets and services we offer to our audience usually fall into one of the following categories:

---

[2] Samuelson, P., & Nordhaus, W. (2006). Economy, 18th Ed. Mexico: McGraw-Hill Interamericana.

a) Necessity assets: consumers require assets or services regardless of how prices move. They will purchase them as usual to continue their daily activities. Some examples are essential food items and gasoline.

These assets have inelastic demand because as the price rises, the proportionate decrease in the quantity demanded by consumers is less than one since they need to buy these products regardless of the price.

b) Luxury assets: these are assets or services that consumers do not require for their daily activities, but instead, they are preferences or desires that only a few can afford due to their economic status or the income they generate. Luxury cars are an asset example. If their prices were more affordable tomorrow, consumers would demand them more because, in these conditions, acquiring an asset generally out of reach becomes possible.

Luxury assets have elastic demand because the quantity demanded varies significantly in response to a price variation. It is advisable to consider this when deciding on product prices and designing offers.

c) Normal assets: Consumers demand assets and services that are less essential for their daily activities. These assets tend to have unitary demand based on consumer behavior. In other words, if the price increases by 2%, the quantity demanded decreases by 2%.

An example of these assets and services is the purchase of ice cream. The product will be consumed similarly whether prices increase or decrease, assuming all other variables remain constant. Unlike the two types of assets or services described earlier, a price decrease will not cause a significant upward spike in the quantity demanded, as would happen with luxury assets. Likewise, an increase in prices will lead to changes in the amount required, unlike what happens with necessity assets. In other words, if the price decreases, people will not consume more ice cream than they usually do. Still, if the price increases, customers will reduce their consumption of ice cream.

Understanding demand elasticity is suggested because our products or services eventually fall into one of these three categories. Not knowing how the target audience behaves can result in a pricing strategy that fails to achieve set goals and objectives.

Once we understand how the quantity demanded of a asset or service is affected and know the factors influencing the amount required, we can envision a scenario where we observe how our consumers interact. This helps us create offers and promotions and set prices based on short- and long-term aspirations.

One of the most common mistakes small business owners make is their need for knowledge regarding the demand elasticity in their target market for their products or services. When determining prices, there needs to be more clarity, considering whether the product or service is a necessity, a luxury item, or a normal asset. As clarified earlier, the demand curve for these assets behaves differently.

Necessity assets usually experience an increase or decrease in the quantity demanded due to factors affecting demand. Business owners must monitor these variables to control the amount required of their products or services and prevent them from decreasing or increasing disproportionately.

While an increase in the quantity demanded would be excellent for our company, we will explain later why, in some situations, producing more could negatively impact net profits, thus reducing the profit margin. Conversely, if we refuse to produce more due to a lack of conditions and preparation (machinery, physical space, labor, among others), we would pave the way for competitors to enter our market and take away our market share.

The price affects necessity assets, but as the name suggests, they are necessary assets that consumers will demand regardless of their price. Multiple competitors in the market offer the same product or service, so if prices were increased, it would likely not be well received by consumers (since there are more providers in the market). This is why competitors in this market tend to focus their efforts more on the quality, quantity, and image of the products to differentiate themselves rather than on price increases or decreases.

On the other hand, in the case of luxury assets, a decrease in the purchase price of the product or service could increase demand. Applying one strategy or another will depend on short and long-term goals.

1.2 Supply

Now that we understand how consumers behave when choosing a asset or service, meaning that we recognize one or several market niches to decide where we will direct our products and services, we must understand the other side: supply. We will evaluate which variables affect the quantity supplied and the incentives to provide or stop giving in a particular market.

As Tucker[3] says, the **Law of Supply** indicates that the quantity supplied positively correlates with the offered price if all variables remain constant. This means that a higher price leads to a greater quantity supplied because producers are more incentivized to provide their products or services. Conversely, if the prices of assets or services decrease, producers or service providers will not be as incentivized to increase their production or services, and as a result, the quantity supplied will decrease.

If we graph the slope, unlike the Law of Demand, which has a negative slope, we will notice that the slope of the Law of Supply is positive, or more precisely, upward.

Now, just like demand, supply is also affected by factors. Knowing these factors is important for making decisions about whether to enter a market niche or sector with such demand. Below, we explain each of these factors.

> **a. Number of sellers**: It is closely related to the demand for products or services, which defines the market size. As the number of competitor's increases, the quantity supplied will be greater. Similarly, as there are fewer competitors in a market, the quantity supplied will be lower.

---

[3] Tucker I.B. (2001). Fundamentals of Economics, 3rd Ed. United States: Thomson Lerning.

We propose taking this into account because if there are many competitors in a market, the buyers will determine the price of the products or services. Increasing the product's price above the average of other suppliers will likely lead to decreased consumption. For these reasons, in a highly competitive market, suppliers focus more on modifying the presentation and quality and highlighting the purpose of their products or services rather than raising or lowering the price.

b. Technology: If new technologies are implemented in the market or sector we are targeting, they will determine how competitive we can be compared to other suppliers. Suppose there is a new technology to reduce production costs, and we do not have access to it, but our competition does. In that case, we will be at a disadvantage. Likewise, the quantity supplied by us may be less than the quantity provided by our competition.

This factor is crucial in highly competitive sectors or countries, as technology constantly changes, and new processes are continually being developed to improve production and reduce costs.

c. price of resources: In economics, there is the concept of "production resources," including (i) capital, (ii) labor, and (iii) land.

As these resources increase in price or, alternatively, if the capital available for work decreases, our quantity will be less than that of our competition with a better system or composition of resources. For example, if we were banana producers exporting to other markets, or if there was increased local demand due to the arrival of tourists demanding the product, we would need new land. If our capital is required to be raised for this purpose or included in our operational plan, we would rent land from other producers to meet the demand for the product.

However, an increase in the price of land for banana production would determine the additional quantity of bananas we would harvest beyond what we already offer. Similarly, an increase in worker wages would increase the cost of production. If the offered asset or service does not allow for an upward price trend, we will decrease the supply to continue offering products that align with the new cost structure.

An increase in the price of resources has a significant impact, as it affects everything we need to carry out our production and offer our services. The effect of increased machinery prices, land costs for production or purchase, labor, and decreased capital, among others, is evident. For this reason, it is crucial to determine the extent to which this variable influences the sector where we set our course.

d. Taxes and subsidies. This variable can positively or negatively influence the sector where we are located. For example, if we were engaged in education, and the country where we are based has laws and incentives for this sector because it prioritizes providing the population with more access to quality education, we could benefit from subsidies to our operations or be exempt from paying certain taxes. This variable would have a positive impact by reducing the costs of our operations. For these reasons, the quantity supplied by us would increase.

On the contrary, if we were in the mining sector and the location where we operate is environmentally affected because the products we need to extract minerals are harmful to nature, and the government establishes taxes to address these externalities, it would decrease the quantity we supply because the production cost of our product, due to the added tax burden, would be higher compared to providing a service in another market. In this scenario, the factor has had a negative impact on our production.

That's why it is crucial to analyze the sector where we are located because depending on the impact or societal needs, governments establish new taxes and exempt or subsidize suppliers to address specific country needs.

e. Producers' expectations. Producers' expectations are closely related to demand expectations. Suppose we speculate about the future behavior of a asset or service. In that case, we will eventually increase or decrease the quantity supplied. In other words, if we know that prices will fall, the amount provided before the price reduction will be higher until it occurs. Similarly, we know that the price of an asset or service will be higher in two weeks. In that case, the quantity supplied before that will lower until the price changes. Thus, the importance of knowing producers' expectations lies in understanding when the quantity supplied will be higher or lower.

f. price of other assets and services. Another factor that affects supply is the price of related assets or substitutes. Suppose the price of those substitute products or services decreases in our market. In that case, it will reduce the quantity supplied since other more affordable products or services are available to meet the demand for the assets or services offered by our company.

The opposite can also occur, meaning related or substitute products significantly increase prices. In this case, we must automatically increase the supply of our products or services to capture the market and meet the existing demand.

We are familiar with the factors affecting the quantity supplied when entering a market or sector. These factors serve as the basis for determining when it is necessary to increase or decrease supply. Therefore, we can continue studying other aspects of supply.

Just as there is elasticity of quantity demanded, there is also elasticity of quantity supplied. This can be: (i) elastic, (ii) inelastic, and (iii) unitary. In general, the elasticity of supply measures the degree to which the quantity supplied responds to a variation in the price of the assets or services. This information can be positive or negative depending on the sector.

In addition to these three types of elasticity of supply, we have the phenomena of **perfectly elastic supply and perfectly inelastic supply**. When supply is perfectly inelastic, regardless of the price of the assets or services, a specific quantity will always be demanded. This occurs when companies consume explicit raw materials to produce their products. On the other hand, a perfectly elastic supply means that the quantity required of that product or service is infinite at one particular price. This indicates that multiple competitors are offering the same thing. If we were to change the price of that product or service, we would be exposed to the possibility of no one consuming what we offer.

1.3 Production Possibilities Frontier

To distinguish certain behaviors, we already know about demand and supply, the factors that influence price differences and the quantity supplied and demanded, and the different types of assets and services in terms of their elasticity. We have identified other sectors of the economy, how consumers respond to market stimuli, and how the market behaves for target audiences. Now, we will learn essential concepts to assess opportunities in markets.

The first thing we need to understand is production possibilities frontiers. Given the availability of resources and technology, they represent the maximum attainable production of a combination of two products or services. If we do not have these resources, they become limiting factors.

Previously, we identified the production resources (labor, land, and capital). Considering these elements in combination with the access to the technology needed for production or service provision allows us to calculate the quantity demanded. This way, we can identify the most efficient areas and focus on that market.

For example, let's say we have a plantation for banana production, and hypothetically, it is also possible to produce other agricultural products, such as sugarcane. However, we need more capital for the machinery required for sugarcane harvesting, or the cost of harvesting and maintaining bananas for supply is higher. By creating a table that details the production possibilities of an asset, we can determine which option is more feasible to plant and decide how much land we will allocate to the production of each product.

Land Quantity	Banana Production	Sugarcane Production
Option A	1,000	0
Option B	800	1,000
Option C	300	3,000
Option D	0	5,000

This allows us to assess which product is more feasible and profitable to cultivate and supply, as one of these options maximizes the invested resources. We perform this analysis to understand which product or service in our sector is most profitable to invest in.

To complement the analysis, we must understand three fundamental points in economics: **scarcity, surplus, and equilibrium point**. These variables reflect the profitability of entering or exiting an economic sector, as they help us examine the market failures into which we want to venture.

Firstly, scarcity occurs when the quantity demanded exceeds the quantity supplied. While this can be attractive for entering a market because the demand for the product or service is already guaranteed, it is essential to confirm why the supply is deficient in this market. Remember that the Law of Supply states that if all other variables remain constant, the quantity supplied decreases as the price drops. This means that there are better investment options than scarcity in a market. Instead, it is crucial to investigate the factors discouraging producers from increasing the supply of assets or services in this market. After this analysis, considering the production possibilities of our business, we can make an informed decision about entering the market.

On the other hand, if there is a surplus in a market due to its opening, meaning that the inventory turnover has slowed down due to an excess supply compared to the quantity demanded, we must verify if the surplus is due to a particular condition and how long it will last. Additionally, we need to determine how long our stored assets can be preserved because if they deteriorate quickly, it would be challenging to maintain the situation for an extended period. In such a case, we would be forced to lower prices to sell the assets before expiration. Suppose the assets can be stored for a prolonged period. In that case, we should assess whether it is profitable to keep them and offer them again when prices return to normal.

Likewise, in most markets, we must be aware of the equilibrium point where suppliers are willing to produce at the price set for their assets, and demanders are eager to consume the quantities offered at the given price. If we are unaware of the equilibrium point in the sector, we may face a shortage of the assets or services we offer. This could be positive as it would ensure the sale of all our merchandise. However, by not meeting the existing demand, we leave open the possibility for our consumers to try substitute products or for new suppliers to enter our market. Additionally, we could have an excess inventory, and costs could multiply, which would not benefit our business.

This analysis aims to ensure that when developing a business idea, we consider all the variables and essential information to enter a sector and possess the necessary information to know when to decrease our participation in a market.

1.4 Costs, Revenues, and Benefits

1.4.1 Business Costs

As mentioned earlier, the book's objective is to provide the reader with a broad understanding of all the factors they need to master to enter a new market or those that influence the market in which they already operate. It also aims to help them understand what they need to comprehend to expand their production or exit the market.

So far, we have addressed the three main economic questions: what to produce, for whom to make, and how to create. Now, we would like to delve into the costs involved in production, how to set prices, and what maximum level of performance could be achieved.

The first thing to understand is that costs encompass all the money outflows incurred to offer a product or service. It is recommended to differentiate costs from expenses, as expenses are the outflows of a business's income to carry out its operations. Expenses include payments for utilities and administrative salaries, among others. We will delve deeper into these concepts later, but for now, let's focus on costs.

Every business starts with an opportunity cost, which is the **cost of sacrificing** one product or service for another, or more precisely, what we forego to make room for other activities. If we take the previous example of the production possibilities frontier, the opportunity cost would be the choice between producing bananas versus sugarcane. We refer to this choice as opportunity cost, as we discard all other options.

Given this, the opportunity cost determines where we will start, that is, how we will produce and which path we will take for our business. It should be taken seriously because capital or production limitations require strict measures to guide the company.

When faced with two asset business options and knowing that the market needs both products and services, but we have limitations to operate both businesses simultaneously, using **comparative advantage** can help determine which one to choose. Our production possibilities frontier would look as follows:

Production based on 8 hours of work	
Production of Shirts	**Production of Pants**
300 units	150 units

Based on the above information, we understand the comparative advantage of producing an asset with a lower opportunity cost than another. We observe that our company foregoes producing two shirts for every pair of pants made. For every shirt made, we forego having 0.5 pants. This means we should focus on creating shirts because, for our factory, the opportunity cost of giving up pants is lower than the opportunity cost of giving up shirts.

Opportunity costs are also referred to as implicit costs. Many decisions for establishing or analyzing an existing business depend on these costs. They operate differently from explicit costs, which are all costs that involve a cash outflow to cover them. They are used to create the operational budget of the business. Among them, we find:
- ✓ Employees' salaries.
- ✓ Insurance.
- ✓ Rentals.
- ✓ Electricity services.
- ✓ Telecommunications services.
- ✓ Fuel.
- ✓ Advertising expenses.

- ✓ Taxes.
- ✓ Maintenance of fixed assets.

We are really interested in studying implicit costs, which do not involve a cash outflow but motivate us to forgo an action or alternative, as explained earlier. Understanding these costs is essential to complement a business's operational budget and make a more informed decision about a business idea.

Within a business's most common implicit costs, we can mention the following actions: using the company's capital or assets and using resources from shareholders, investors, or business owners.

For example, consider a factory that produces pens for mass consumption, allowing large corporations to promote their brands by giving them as gifts to their clients. In this factory, there are three trucks: two are used to acquire the materials for pen production, and a smaller truck is used to deliver customer orders. The business operates in two locations, one being the production facility housing the machinery in an industrial warehouse. Another industrial warehouse stores materials and assets and dispatches orders to customers in the exact location. The administrative offices are situated in the other location. The business occupies two levels of a building owned by a proprietor who has contributed to the company's operations. The building has six levels of corporate offices, all of which have been occupied.

The implicit costs we will examine for the business are as follows:
1. Leasing costs for the trucks used by the company.
2. Leasing costs for the industrial warehouse for storage.
3. Leasing costs for the administrative offices.

Combining implicit costs requires us to analyze the business from a different perspective. For instance, if we request our suppliers to deliver the materials to our facilities, we could have two trucks available for other activities—leasing them to generate additional income or selling them to capitalize on operations. Another possibility would be for customers to pick up their orders from our facilities instead of us delivering them.

Here, we contemplate the following variables:
- ✓ What would capitalizing on the two additional trucks mean for our business?
- ✓ How much would our suppliers charge us additionally to deliver the materials?
- ✓ What added value would delivering the assets to our customers represent?
- ✓ How many customers would be willing to pick up their products from our facilities?

These inquiries make sense, as they account for a business's implicit costs. It's not just about looking at costs that involve a cash outflow.

On the other hand, there are the implicit costs of administrative offices and assets storage. After calculating feasibility, an option is to eliminate the administrative offices and move them to the merchandise storage area.

These combinations lead to evaluating how much the owner could earn by leasing the two corporate floors that house the administrative offices and how much the company makes by producing based on orders to avoid storage. If we proceed this way, we will have the following changes in our operational structure, provided that all necessary analyses have been conducted:

1- There would be a reduced fixed cost, as the machines would only be turned on to meet customer needs, not to maintain a selected assets inventory
2- . Employee payroll would also be reduced, as inventory management would require no personnel.

3- The company would invest working capital in maintaining an inventory of assets.
4- It would also have better control over all operations, as they would all be located in the exact location.
5- The owner would earn income from leasing the two floors occupied by administrative offices.

The alternatives provided by implicit costs allow us to examine the business model and propose viable options that are more profitable as long as the value chain is not compromised. Similarly, we are considering a new business. In that case, this analysis allows us to include all possible options in the budget to make operations more efficient and generate more income without affecting the quality of our products or services.

Based on everything discussed above, the correct way to analyze the economic benefits produced by our business model is by comparing total revenues with implicit and explicit costs. This way, we can make a well-informed decision about the direction of the business. Typically, only explicit costs (cash outflows) are considered, as shown in the following graph.

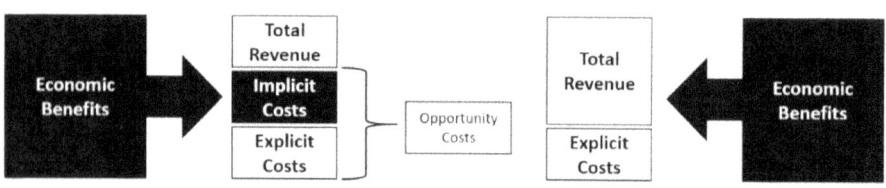

On the other hand, we encounter **fixed costs** and **variable costs**. Fixed costs of a business are all the costs that we incur that do not change as production changes, and they have to be paid even if the decision we make is not to produce anything. This includes expenses like rent and property insurance, among others. In contrast, variable costs are all the costs directly involved with production, meaning that if production increases or decreases, costs also increase or decrease. This includes expenses such as labor, electricity, raw materials, and others. The sum of these costs gives us **the total production cost**, allowing us to understand precisely how costs increase as the assets to be offered are produced.

Understanding these three costs (variable, fixed, and total) is crucial for studying production as a whole and determining the **average cost per unit** and the **marginal cost**. These must be considered to calculate our quantities, regardless of the industry or sector we enter. By understanding these concepts, we can define what is more feasible regarding production. We also realize that having a higher quantity of assets doesn't necessarily lead to lower costs. There's a point on the curve where continuing production does not maximize the organization's profits.

As the name suggests, the **average cost or cost per unit** is the result of dividing the total cost by the quantity produced. We analyze all the costs and calculate the average cost to understand the contribution of each cost when extending production. This means we need to consider the average variable cost, fixed cost, and total cost, as they provide a more comprehensive view of how costs fluctuate as we produce more quantity. They also indicate how these costs decrease, helping us determine a point where returns are maximized.

As mentioned earlier, **marginal cost** refers to the cost of producing one more unit or analyzing the cost of the last unit produced. Its formula is based on dividing the change in total cost by the change in the unit produced.

Below, we will explain in more detail how these costs are examined.

Total Production	Fixed Cost	Variable Cost	Total Cost	Average Fixed Cost	Average Variable Cost	Average Total Cost	Marginal Cost
0	$100	$0	$100				
1	$100	$50	$150	$100	$50	$150	$50
2	$100	$80	$180	$50	$40	$90	$30
3	$100	$100	$200	$33	$33	$67	$20
4	$100	$120	$220	$25	$30	$55	$20
5	$100	$150	$250	$20	$30	$50	$30
6	$100	$180	$280	$17	$30	$47	$30
7	$100	$220	$320	$14	$31	$46	$40
8	$100	$270	$370	$13	$34	$46	$50
9	$100	$330	$430	$11	$37	$48	$60
10	$100	$400	$500	$10	$40	$50	$70
11	$100	$500	$600	$9	$45	$55	$100
12	$100	$620	$720	$8	$52	$60	$120

According to the table, the total cost of production always increases as we produce more items. However, we genuinely want to know the unit cost of production to make rational decisions for our business. Consequently, it's noticeable that the average variable cost in production number 7 increases, and each additional output is more expensive than producing the previous quantities.

This occurs due to factors involved in production, such as machinery, technology, and labor, among others. As production increases, we encounter certain limitations. For these reasons, increasing labor is not profitable if we don't have the necessary machinery to operate. The idle hours of each worker would be higher, which is a valid reason for the average variable cost to start rising instead of continuing to decrease after a certain point.

We notice that the average total cost rises when our production reaches 9. In that case, everything produced before that quantity is theoretically efficient. To test this theory, we calculate the marginal cost, which tells us the cost of the last unit produced. This allows us to validate that production eight does not maximize the company's profits because its cost is higher than production 7. For these reasons, it's ideal for our business to produce items up to production 7 to obtain the highest returns on investment.

1.4.2 Revenue Generation

Revenues are determined by the quantity sold and the price at which we sell the assets. It is essential to know how to estimate the best price based on the elasticity of the assets or services we offer, consumer behavior, and the composition of the supply market.

This section will not discuss setting prices or pricing strategies. Instead, we will learn about the **average and marginal revenue** of our products.

Revenue is the money inflow our business receives based on the quantity we offer and what consumers purchase. Consequently, if we talk about average revenue, we refer to the cash inflow per unit we sell in the market. On the other hand, we have marginal revenue, which expresses the income generated from the sale of an additional unit of production. As shown in the table below, we calculate it by dividing the change in total revenue from one production batch to another by the change in units produced in that batch.

For example, the total revenue from the production of one unit is $60. When we produce two units, the total revenue is $120. Therefore, the difference in total revenue between the two productions is $60, and the units had increased from 1 to 2, which is a difference of one unit.

The equation would be $60/1 = $60.

Total Production	Total Cost	Total Revenue	Profits	Marginal Cost	Marginal Revenue
0	$100	0	($100)		
1	$150	$60	($90)	$50	$60
2	$180	$120	($60)	$30	$60
3	$200	$180	($20)	$20	$60
4	$220	$240	$20	$20	$60
5	$250	$300	$50	$30	$60
6	$280	$360	$80	$30	$60
7	$320	$420	$100	$40	$60
8	$370	$480	$110	$50	$60
9	$430	$540	$110	$60	$60
10	$500	$600	$100	$70	$60
11	$600	$660	$60	$100	$60
12	$720	$720	$0	$120	$60

From the above table, we can conclude that:

a) Producing less than three items results in losses for the company as we fail to cover the total production costs.

b) Producing nine items doesn't yield profits since marginal cost and marginal revenue are equal. Therefore, it doesn't add value to our operations.

c) Producing any quantity beyond nine results in losses because marginal revenue is less than marginal cost. Each additional item produced fails to maximize shareholder income.

d) The optimal level to produce with this framework is four items because that's where the highest profit lies. However, we can produce up to six items and achieve asset returns.

We will know the production levels we can achieve depending on the profit levels we establish in our business. Remember that profits result from subtracting total income from total costs incurred.

After understanding the concepts of cost, revenue, and profit, identifying the production point that maximizes our business's benefits allows us to devise strategies by applying **economies of scale** and **economies of scope**.

Economies of scale occur when costs decrease as we produce more units, meaning the average total cost per unit falls. In this case, we study whether having an additional "x" amount results in a lower cost than producing "x" products.

We introduced this concept after learning about marginal cost and marginal revenue because while it's true that costs decrease with increased production, we need to be aware of up to what point we can reduce costs with more production within our business model. As previously mentioned, there's a point where extending production leads to cost increases rather than reductions.

Next, we present an example of economies of scale. Let's examine the production of pens in our factory. We produce a larger quantity, reducing average costs per unit.

Pens	100	200	300	400	500	600
Blue Pens	$30.00	$50.00	$70.00	$89.00	$105.00	$120.00
Black Pens	$25.00	$55.00	$90.00	$125.00	$160.00	$200.00
Red Pens	$35.00	$55.00	$80.00	$120.00	$155.00	$190.00

To prepare the economy of scale analysis, we proceed to divide the average total cost by the quantities produced, which gives us the following graph:

Pens	100	200	300	400	500	600
Blue Pens	$0.30	$0.25	$0.23	$0.22	$0.21	$0.20
Black Pens	$0.25	$0.28	$0.30	$0.31	$0.32	$0.33
Red Pens	$0.35	$0.28	$0.27	$0.30	$0.31	$0.32

As we can see with blue pens, producing a more significant quantity leads to decreased cost per unit, indicating that economies of scale are being employed in making this pen. Regarding red pens, initially, they exhibit a behavior similar to that of blue pens. Still, when production reaches 400 units, the price continues to rise. Since the cost per unit at the end of the output of 600 pens is lower than the cost of producing 100 pens, the efficiency in the economies of scale for this product is achieved by having 300 units. This economies of scale analysis, combined with marginal cost and revenue, helps us gain insight into where we can be more efficient in production and generate more profitability.

Economies of scope, on the other hand, refer to producing other products from the raw materials we already have. For instance, if we make mints, we can manufacture lollipops, as they essentially use the same materials. This way, we diversify our product portfolio. However, as we've learned, there's an opportunity cost, and we must examine how much to produce for each product. This is because our production possibilities frontier will limit the quantity we have.

CHAPTER II: ACCOUNTING

In this chapter, I aim not to turn you into an accountant but rather to equip you with the essential knowledge to understand the business's financial information, as it is the language of companies. It is the means through which we communicate our financial well-being and focus on improving our situation. Companies often close due to a need to properly understand the business's financial information. The absence of internal controls creates vulnerabilities in the health of our organization, and funds start to deviate from their intended path.

In a nutshell, the company's accounting helps us comprehend the financial situation of our business to make informed decisions and evaluate the progress of the business idea we are developing. Furthermore, financial information plays a pivotal role in entering the market and securing funds for project development. This information allows us to access financing and investment channels like banks, investment funds, investors, stock exchanges, and other market participants.

2.1 Basic Items of Financial Statements

In this section, we will learn about the fundamental items and their interpretation, basic financial statements, the most significant financial ratios for measuring the effectiveness of our execution, and essential appendices to understand financial information. This will enable us to comprehend the financial information of our business but also interpret information from other businesses, as we have rightly indicated that it is the universal language of business.

2.1.1 Definitions and Basic Concepts

We will now proceed to introduce the concepts of the essential items in financial statements that are recommended to be understood to grasp their content.

a. Assets: These are tangible and intangible resources a business possesses to conduct its operations. They are classified into two major groups: (a) **current assets**, which are assets that can be converted into cash within a year or less, and (b) **fixed assets**, which are assets that take longer than a year to convert into cash. This categorization organizes assets based on their level of liquidity conversion, meaning how easily an asset can be converted into cash.

b. Liabilities: These are the internal (debts to shareholders) or external obligations and debts of a business that support a portion of the company's assets. They are categorized by time frames: (a) **current liabilities**, which are debts or obligations settled within a year or less, and (b) **long-term liabilities**, which encompass the company's debts with terms exceeding a year.

c. Equity or Capital: These are the resources shareholders contribute to initiating the business, along with profits accumulated in previous periods and the current management, supporting a portion of the company's assets.

Based on the definitions above, the basic accounting equation is: **Assets = Liabilities + Equity**.

d. Statement of Financial Position or Balance Sheet: Each transaction recorded in the company has a corresponding entry to substantiate the operation. These account groups constitute the Statement of Financial Position or Balance Sheet, providing a snapshot of the period under analysis to discern the execution up to that point.

e. Income Statement or Profit and Loss Statement: This presents the revenue inflows and expense outflows generated in the business. Using this financial statement, we measure profits based on expenditures and adjust items for greater efficiency.

f. Revenues: These encompass all cash inflows a business receives from sales of services or products.

g. Expenses: These encompass all cash outflows made by a company to deliver sales or services to customers. These items are categorized as follows:

- **Cost of Assets Sold**: These are the production or acquisition costs of the products a company sells.
- **Administrative Expenses**: These are expenses incurred by the company to support daily operations, such as electricity payments, security services, administrative staff salaries, and communication costs, among others.
- **Selling Expenses**: These are expenses related to marketing and selling a company's products and/or services, such as salespeople's salaries, commission payments, and advertising costs, among others.
- **Financial Expenses**: These are banking and economic costs incurred by a company for cash management or financing its operations. They

often include account management fees, bank statement fees, financing interest, and bank commissions, among others.

In this context, it's worth noting that there are two fundamental Financial Statements: (a) Cash Flow Statement, which shows cash inflows and outflows over a given period based on operating financing and investing activities, and (b) Statement of Changes in Equity, which reports changes in the company's equity over a predetermined period.

For the purposes of this book, we will focus on two Financial Statements: the Balance Sheet and the Income Statement. In these times, operations have become more complex and competitive, necessitating an understanding of business procedures and executing actions aligned with the strategic plan to achieve the desired performance in commercial activities.

2.1.2 Current Assets

As specified earlier, a business's assets are tangible and intangible resources to conduct its operations. There are two significant groups: current assets and fixed assets.

Current assets are typically composed of items such as: (i) cash, cash equivalents, and bank accounts; (ii) accounts receivable; (iii) inventory; (iv) investments; and (v) prepaid expenses.

Hence, it's not just about knowing which items constitute current assets but also understanding how these items are managed and maintaining controls to prevent cash leaks in the company. These are the only resources available for day-to-day operations, making up the company's working capital. Given their importance, let's analyze the first three items of current assets.

i. Cash in Cash and Bank

This item represents physical money reserved for short-term obligations. It's crucial to ensure the following questions are addressed:
   a) Is prior authorization required for cash disbursements?
   b) Have functions like authorization, selection, sales, custody, collection, and treasury been adequately segregated?
   c) Are bank reconciliations conducted at regular intervals?
   d) Do we possess reports on income and expense records and controls?
   e) Are mechanisms in place to ensure accurate recording of deposits?

These are basic inquiries concerning controls over cash in petty cash and bank accounts. Besides verifying the responses to these questions, it's beneficial to incorporate the following measures:
   ✓ Segregate responsibilities of those handling cash.
   ✓ Establish procedures for payments, transaction control, and accounting record-keeping.
   ✓ Separate duties of petty cash handlers and collection handlers.
   ✓ Entrust authorization for minor cash expenses to a person different from its handler.
   ✓ Conduct regular audits of the company's little cash.
   ✓ Issue checks in consecutive order.
   ✓ Issue invoices and receipts sequentially.

These measures will prevent leaks in petty cash. Small and medium-sized businesses often need more control in this area. Due to the relatively low funds they handle, many companies need to pay more attention to this aspect. Sometimes, they only realize the situation after several years of consistent cash leaks.

Another reason aligning processes from the outset is recommended is that most businesses develop processes as they mature. However, growth is only sometimes controlled; there are leaps and bounds, referred to as opportunities, where a company can triple or even quadruple its operations. Without crucial elements and control processes, there is a risk of losses due to not organizing the business operations from the beginning.

ii. Accounts Receivable

From the moment a business starts, the market demands that we extend credit to frequent customers or those who make substantial purchases. All sales should be cash-only, and credit should only be extended to customers who require it for a maximum of 30 days.

It's essential to be very cautious about this, as poor management can leave the company without the necessary cash flow for day-to-day operations. Cash flow problems can manifest as reduced inventory or delayed payment of obligations. To address this, if we offer credit, it's suggested that we devise a mechanism that ensures cash recovery. The recovered amount comes with an additional dividend to cover the customer's financing cost during that period.

For example, consider the following scenario: We obtain a credit line to finance accounts receivable or inventory due to a working capital deficit. This line incurs an interest rate of 15% annually for $1 million, resulting in an annual interest of $150,000. With the bank credit, we managed to purchase 10,000 items. In this case, we need to increase the cost of the products by $15 to cover the interest and increase it by $100 to cover the direct cost of purchasing. As we had to finance operations due to lack of capital, an additional $15 is added to the cost of products, which helps avoid seeking additional financing if we are asked for credit.

Since this is the cost of financing in the current context, it's advised to offer terms with early payment discounts, ensuring cash collection within 30 days. Similarly, we can offer discounts for prompt payments, removing the additional charge mentioned earlier. In any case, the important thing is to assign an interest cost to the products we will finance for our customers, based on the current rate of financial institutions, so that our accounts receivable can cover the cost we would incur if we were to take additional credit.

Many businesses do not consider this and sacrifice their favorable margins, as customers who extend credit exceed the granted terms. What we propose is a healthy way to mitigate risk.

In addition to the charges mentioned, late fees should be considered for customers who exceed the credit period. If a customer pays after the given days, we'll likely experience a reduction in the return the product provides. Ultimately, the operation may result in losses rather than profits, as there comes a point where the recovered money doesn't yield benefits and falls below the current cost of the merchandise.

iii. Inventory

This section won't delve into how to account for or which cost method is most suitable for your business. Instead, we'll emphasize the value of internal inventory control for reporting purposes and safeguarding assets while highlighting the importance of maintaining optimal inventory levels.

Inventories have a cost to acquire, meaning they represent cash outflows. An increase from year to year reduces a business's liquidity; a decrease from year to year represents cash inflows that enhance a company's liquidity. For this reason, keeping inventory turnover at optimal levels is crucial—meaning how many times inventory moves within a year.

When we perform the calculation, we often realize that inventory turnover is 270 days, indicating that the merchandise moves only some of the time. As with timber, this slow turnover is only favorable if the product is scarce for specific periods. Cutting occurs during particular times of the year (and not other periods), so traders prefer to expand their inventory to meet demand during scarcity.

However, if we're not in an industry with these characteristics, we face the following disadvantages:
- ✓ Less-than-optimal liquidity due to inventory leverage.
- ✓ Inventory obsolescence.
- ✓ Deterioration of assets due to storage.
- ✓ Increased risk of loss due to various factors (theft, pests, natural events, etc.).

Ideally, we should project expected sales for the current year and adjust inventory, considering the time it takes to procure merchandise. This way, we can maintain low inventory levels, thereby enhancing liquidity for daily business operations or making investments in case of excess liquidity.

Effective inventory control is crucial, meaning appropriate tools should be adopted to monitor every outgoing or incoming item, thus minimizing losses. Along these lines, the following documents are recommended to improve inventory control:
- ✓ Purchase Order: Authorization for supplier inventory purchases after reviewing and justifying the increase or entry of assets.
- ✓ Receipt Report: Initial entries made to inventory by purchase orders and supplier invoices. The entry record should include minimum requirements such as item description, quantity ordered, and item cost.
- ✓ Supplier Invoice: The invoice provided by suppliers before purchase orders. This invoice should match the purchase order.

With these essential elements, we can control the assets entering our business. We have a purchase order for what we need and an entry report that should match what our suppliers billed and what our company authorized.

To safeguard assets once they're in our business, consider the following measures:
- ✓ Restricted access to authorized personnel, suppliers, and customers.
- ✓ Security cameras are placed for inventory monitoring.
- ✓ Labels or barcodes for traceability of movement for each item.
- ✓ Valuable merchandise is stored under lock and key with limited access.

Depending on business size, these essential measures can help prevent inventory leaks. Sometimes, it's not about theft but about assets being swapped for defective ones, causing us to incur losses by assuming the supplier sent faulty merchandise or the merchandise might be incomplete.

It's also essential to note that stored merchandise should be adequately protected. It's worth considering insuring it, as this item often constitutes a substantial portion of a business's assets and is crucial for continued operations if the company sells products. Many don't see the need to insure their assets due to a lack of awareness about their importance. Additionally, storage areas could be better, causing long-term damage and significant losses to the company.

Like cash, inventories should be reviewed periodically, and physical counts should be conducted to verify that the merchandise matches the reports. To be accurate, these counts should be random and not communicated to staff in advance.

After the review, generating a new report is advisable to compare previous information and determine what we still have. It's possible to discover obsolete merchandise in the inventory, which incurs losses for the business or items about to expire, allowing us to sell them before incurring losses. There may also be damaged products due to poor storage. For these and other reasons, a physical review is recommended to produce a new inventory report that is more accurate and reflective of reality.

Having analyzed the most significant items in current assets where we should focus efforts for more effective operations, we'll move on to **fixed assets**. This isn't to say that the other items are unimportant. Still, controls for those items are easier to manage and don't represent notable cash leaks.

2.1.3 Fixed Assets

The essential items that make up fixed assets are as follows:
- Furniture and work equipment.
- Vehicles and machinery.
- Buildings and premises.
- Land.

The business uses these assets to carry out its operations. They encompass vehicles used for transporting assets or salespeople, office furniture and work equipment, the land where the office, warehouse, or premises are located, and the buildings used for operations or customer service, among others.

It's important to carefully evaluate the feasibility of acquiring these assets at certain times. Analyze how essential it is to purchase a property, which could lead to the company becoming undercapitalized when there might be another option, such as renting the space. With monthly returns, a suitable rent payment that aligns better with the business's reality could be made. In the end, it's suggested to determine if the investment will benefit the company, as substantial investments that don't result in increased sales or operational improvement are often undertaken. These actions often reflect a desire for these assets rather than an essential business need.

2.1.4 Liabilities and Capital

As mentioned earlier, liabilities are obligations and debts the company has incurred to sustain its regular operations or are part of its normal operations. On the other hand, capital consists of shareholder contributions plus profits from previous and current periods. Essentially, these items support assets, and the fundamental accounting equation states that assets equal liabilities plus capital (assets = liabilities + capital).

The most common items in these categories include:

Current Liabilities:
- Accounts payable
- Lines of credit
- Current portion of long-term debt
- Short-term notes payable
- Taxes payable

Long-Term Liabilities:
- Long-term notes payable
- Long-term loans

Capital:
- Issued shares
- Reserves
- Shareholder contributions
- Profits from previous periods
- Profits from the current period

2.2. Balance Sheet

The Balance Sheet, as the name implies, presents a snapshot of the business on a specific date. It's one of the four most important financial statements to decide the company's future.

The items can be categorized on the balance sheet as follows:

Current Assets:
- Cash, cash equivalents, and bank accounts
- Accounts receivable
- Inventories
- Investments
- Prepaid expenses

Total Current Assets

Fixed Assets:
- Furniture and work equipment
- Vehicles and machinery
- Buildings and premises
- Land

Total Fixed Assets

TOTAL ASSETS (Current Assets + Fixed Assets)

Current Liabilities:
- Accounts payable
- Lines of credit
- Current portion of long-term debt
- Short-term notes payable
- Taxes payable

Total Current Liabilities

Long-Term Liabilities:
- Long-term notes payable
- Long-term loans

Total Long-Term Liabilities

TOTAL LIABILITIES (Current Liabilities + Long-Term Liabilities)

Capital:
- Issued shares
- Reserves
- Shareholder contributions
- Profits from previous periods
- Profits from the current period

Total Capital

TOTAL CAPITAL AND LIABILITIES

It's crucial to understand how to interpret the Balance Sheet to adjust items and make decisions that enhance the business financial health business's financial health. Ideally, you should review the Balance Sheet quarterly and avoid the mistake of inspecting it only annually.

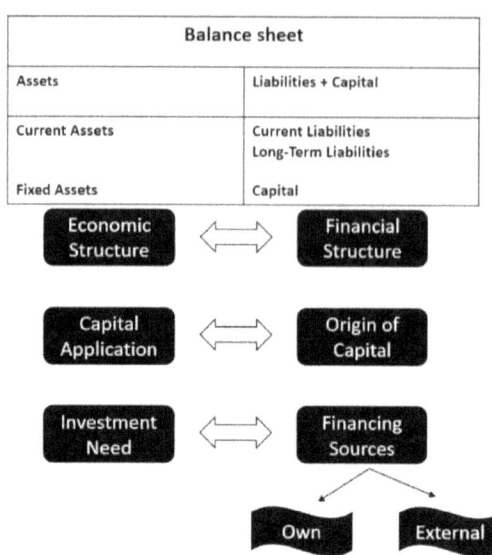

2.3. Financial Ratios from the Balance Sheet

Financial statements allow us to examine our information and interpret it to confirm how it aligns with our business idea and its execution. With the Balance Sheet, we analyze the financial indicators presented below.

2.3.1 Liquidity Ratios

Liquidity ratios measure our ability to meet short-term obligations. They comprise our current liabilities, such as suppliers, taxes, and loan installments, among others.

There are four fundamental financial indicators for this analysis.

- **Working Capital:** This is the capital that companies have for their daily operations, i.e., to meet short-term obligations.

  Current Assets – Current Liabilities

- **Current Ratio:** This ratio is obtained by dividing existing assets by current liabilities. It indicates the degree to which we can meet short-term obligations to our creditors. This ratio is general. It determines the absolute liquidity index and makes more accurate decisions regarding short-term debt or inventory reduction.

    Current Assets / Current Liabilities

- **Quick Ratio (Acid-Test Ratio):** This liquidity ratio indicates what we have to meet short-term creditor obligations without involving inventory. It measures our ability to handle short-term debt with available liquid assets. This ratio is more accurate because it indicates what we actually have to pay obligations and what measures we need to take.

    (Current Assets – Inventory) / Current Liabilities

- **Working Capital Leverage:** This indicator clarifies how much working capital is tied up in inventory. It provides the necessary tools to make informed decisions about the company's liquidity in relation to the inventory item.

    Inventory / (Current Assets – Current Liabilities)

From the above, we start with available liquid assets to meet short-term obligations and then proceed to calculate our level or degree of liquidity. Next, we figure out how to handle these obligations without involving inventory, and finally, we assess how committed working capital is to inventory.

These liquidity indicators are essential for making decisions about business operations. They help us determine if we have the capacity to take on short-term debt, whether we need more working capital to continue projects, or if we should reduce inventory for more liquidity, among other decisions for business execution.

2.3.2 Leverage Ratios

These financial indicators help us understand how committed the company is to creditors and what percentage is in their hands. This indicator is essential because, depending on negotiations, creditors place interest on the financed amount, causing financing costs. This could lead to reduced liquidity for short-term payments.

The leading indicators include:

- **Debt-to-assets ratio**: This leverage indicator considers what portion of creditors have financed assets. It shows what part of operations is supported by financing.
$$\text{Total Debt / Total Assets}$$

- **Leverage Ratio:** This financial ratio studies the relationship between creditor funds and shareholder funds. It helps us understand if the company has the capital to face debt or how much capital is committed to creditors.
$$\text{Total Debt / Total Equity}$$

- **Long-Term Debt to Total Equity Ratio:** This indicator reviews the company's capacity to handle long-term debt or confront it.
$$\text{Long-Term Debt / Total Equity}$$

2.4. Income Statement

The Income Statement helps us understand the performance (profits or losses) of operations over some time. It's a valuable introductory financial statement that reflects the company's revenues, costs, and expenses, allowing us to estimate items according to projections and align them with the business strategy.

The essential items that make up this financial statement include:

Revenues
Sales
(Sales Discounts and Returns)
Total Revenues
Cost of Assets Sold
Gross Profit
General and Administrative Expenses
Selling Expenses
Operating Profit
Financial Expenses
Profit before Taxes
Tax Deductions
Net Profit

There are financial ratios that connect both financial statements (inventory turnover, accounts receivable turnover, return on assets) to measure business profitability and operational efficiency.

By involving the costs and expenses the company incurs, the Income Statement makes it easier to make decisions to reduce them, allowing us to maximize business revenue.

2.4.1 Profitability Ratios

In the structure of the Income Statement, we find various profits before reaching net profit. This allows us to measure efficiency in each of the company's processes. For example, understanding gross profit indicates the percentage of sales represented by costs. This can prompt us to consider alternative suppliers or analyze components (raw materials, direct labor, and manufacturing overhead) for cost reduction.

Similarly, operating profit indicates profit after deducting administrative and general expenses. This section includes items like administrative payroll and service expenses (electricity, phone, water, rent, etc.), among other recurring expenses. This helps us examine their distribution and identify areas for improvement.

The exact process is followed for a profit before taxes. We examine the financial expenses incurred or additional income generated to see how to improve. Gradually, we investigate where we are overspending or incurring extraordinary costs and make corrections to achieve expected profits.

Other ratios or indicators include:

- **Return on Sales (ROS):** This tells us what percentage of sales represents our net income.
$$\text{Net Profit / Sales}$$
- **Return on Equity (ROE):** This indicator studies the income earned by the capital shareholders invest, showing how much return the investment placed in the business has generated.
$$\text{Net Profit / Shareholder's Equity}$$

2.4.2 Operational Ratios

Below, we present various operational indicators.

- **Inventory Turnover:** This indicator analyzes how often inventory has moved during the year, confirming whether we have excess merchandise. Suppose inventory only turns over once in 360 days, and market behavior doesn't warrant it. In that case, we should consider purchasing less inventory to utilize its liquidity.

The inventory turnover formula is as follows:

Inventory Turnover
Cost of Assets Sold / Average Inventory

Monthly Inventory Turnover
12 months / Inventory Turnover

Daily Inventory Turnover
365 days / Inventory Turnover

- **Average Collection Period:** This indicator calculates the time required to receive payment for customer credit sales. It's relevant as it shows how long it takes to realize accounts receivable.

Accounts Receivable / Average Daily Sales

- **Accounts Receivable Turnover:** This indicator tells us how many times we collect accounts receivable in a year or how many times this item has turned over.

Accounts Receivable Turnover

Sales / Average Accounts Receivable

Monthly Accounts Receivable Turnover

12 months / Accounts Receivable Turnover

Daily Accounts Receivable Turnover

365 days / Accounts Receivable Turnover

As mentioned earlier, the importance of financial statements lies in the interpretation we construct from them. This allows us to meaningfully validate their information about our business and apply fundamental measures to align with our strategic plan. Financial statements are the thermometer measuring the state of operations, preventing us from realizing at year-end that we couldn't effectively execute the plan.

Well-prepared financial statements serve as guides and maps for achieving our objectives. Many businesses need more financial information and rely solely on income as they go along. They need to gain the skill to make quick decisions based on parameters. The conclusion needs to be revised because insufficient liquidity isn't necessarily due to high costs or expenses. As we saw earlier, there are efficiency-related items that can guide us to focus our efforts.

2.5. Cash Flow

An aspect to consider in businesses is the ability to predict monthly income flows and ensure that the flow aligns with the business reality. This enables us to make future estimations or projections based on the same.

To calculate our business's income flows, we must address specific company policies regarding sales, collections, and accounts payable. Based on these policies, we can understand how our income flow will be month after month, create projections, examine its behavior (in the case of an established company), and evaluate how it has been fulfilled according to the company's policies.

The sales policy advises measuring the portion of our sales that will be on credit and the portion expected to be received in cash. From this variable, along with the company's sales projection, we infer how its future flows will be.

In collections management, it is suggested to stipulate the number of credit days offered to customers and the collection strategy to be executed, such as whether we will apply discounts for early payment or if there will be penalties for late payment.

In treating accounts payable, we examine agreements with suppliers and their behavior, meaning whether they grant us credit for 30 or 60 days and how their fulfillment is (whether paid before or precisely on the predetermined dates) to estimate projections.

Next, we present an example of a projected income flow for a company from January to December. It is a chocolate distributor with monthly sales of $100,000 and an estimated growth of 2%. 45% of sales are made on 30 days credit, with a 15% early payment discount. 30% of customers have taken advantage of this discount in the last 12 months. Monthly orders are placed with suppliers for $40,000, with a 45-day payment period for the merchandise. Monthly expenses amount to $10,000.

We will assume that accounts payable are settled at the end of the previous period so that we will start with the available credit.

Income Flow Diagram

Details	January	February	March	April	May	June	July	August	September	October	November	December
Sales Growth	2,000.00	2,040.00	2,080.80	2,122.42	2,164.86	2,208.16	2,252.32	2,297.37	2,343.32	2,390.19	2,437.99	2,486.75
Estimated sales	102,000.00	104,040.00	106,120.80	108,243.22	110,408.08	112,616.24	114,868.57	117,165.94	119,509.26	121,899.44	124,337.43	126,824.18
Total Monthly Sales	104,000.00	106,080.00	108,201.60	110,365.63	112,572.94	114,824.40	117,120.89	119,463.31	121,852.58	124,289.63	126,775.42	129,310.93
Sales revenue	56,100.00	57,222.00	58,366.44	59,533.77	60,724.44	61,938.93	63,177.71	64,441.27	65,730.09	67,044.69	68,385.59	69,753.30
Income Accounts Collecting		45,900.00	46,818.00	47,754.36	48,709.45	49,683.64	50,677.31	51,690.86	52,724.67	53,779.17	54,854.75	55,951.84
Total Monthly Income	56,100.00	103,122.00	105,184.44	107,288.13	109,433.89	111,622.57	113,855.02	116,132.12	118,454.76	120,823.86	123,240.34	125,705.14
Fixed costs	10,000.00	10,000.00	10,000.00	10,000.00	10,000.00	10,000.00	10,000.00	10,000.00	10,000.00	10,000.00	10,000.00	10,000.00
Accounts payable		40,000.00	40,000.00		40,000.00	40,000.00		40,000.00	40,000.00		40,000.00	40,000.00
Total Monthly Expenses	10,000.00	50,000.00	50,000.00	10,000.00	50,000.00	50,000.00	10,000.00	50,000.00	50,000.00	10,000.00	50,000.00	50,000.00
Income Flow	46,100.00	53,122.00	55,184.44	97,288.13	59,433.89	61,622.57	103,855.02	66,132.12	68,454.76	110,823.86	73,240.34	75,705.14
Average Flow	72,580.00											

According to the graph, the company's income flow is variable, and we can use short-term funds for both investments in profitable instruments and unforeseen situations. The importance of income flow is that we have a projection of how the company's income is generated to use appropriately.

CHAPTER III: STRATEGIC PLAN AND EXECUTION

The most essential part of a business is its strategic plan, which serves as a map with directions on how we will achieve our purpose. Unfortunately, many companies lack a well-designed map and operate on the go. We notice how some companies evolve faster than others in the same sector, and it's simply due to their strategic planning to achieve the set aspiration.

Most businesses only have a definition of their target market and an idea of how they plan to reach it or how they will distribute their products. This need to analyze other intervening variables and how to execute them is what makes the difference in success between companies.

Typically, this occurs with small and medium-sized businesses that arise out of necessity or shareholders' desire to enter a sector they're passionate about. This passion or need to generate extra income often leads them to not inquire enough about the industry they're entering. As they progress, they add a path to prosperity to their vision. However, they rarely develop a business idea with a clear strategy and execution from the beginning.

In this chapter, we will help you recognize the factors that compose the strategic plan, the most substantial variables, and how to execute it. Therefore, this is the real difference in why some show positive trends, others are stuck where they started, and others lose market positioning.

Suppose you already have your business running and still need a well-defined strategic plan. In that case, you can still design one that takes the company to the next level, incorporating variables that were left out of the original business strategy and figuring out how to execute the strategy effectively.

3.1 What is Strategy?

Kluyver, in his book *"Strategic Thinking: A Perspective for Executives,"* [4] indicates that strategy is about positioning an organization to achieve a sustainable competitive advantage. He states that we must confidently answer three questions:
- Who should I target as customers? Who are my customers?
- What products or services should I offer them? How should I do it?

Creating a strategy aims to add value to shareholders and other interested parties (such as customers), satisfying their needs and desires. For this reason, Constantino C. Makides, author of *"Success is in the Strategy,"* [5] explains that "a superior strategy consists of finding and exploiting a unique strategic position in the company's business while continuously seeking new options."

The business strategy is not only conceived when a business is created. Still, it should be reviewed and modified regularly as our market changes in tastes and preferences differ over the years. Unless we continuously improve, we lose strength over time and stop adding value, making the company obsolete.

A well-crafted strategy covers the following points:
- ✓ How do you form a unique strategic position in the business?
- ✓ How can an established business discover a new strategic position when its operations are profitable?
- ✓ How does the company know if its adopted position will be profitable?
- ✓ Even if the company establishes a strategic position, can it improve two positions simultaneously, the old and the new? Is this possible, or should it concentrate on one of the two?

---

[4] Kluyver, C. A. (2001). Strategic Thinking, a perspective for executives. Buenos Aires: Pearson Education.
[5] Markides, C. C. (2002). Success is in the strategy. Bogotá: Grupo Editorial Norma.

The market behaves like a spiral that constantly turns, causing new strategic positions for current participants and newcomers entering the sector. Accordingly, new combinations of the "who-what-how" are created due to:

- Limitations and developments of current companies regarding their capacity.
- Entry of new competitors offering improved or different products.
- Changes in consumer taste, preference, and needs.
- Changes in regulations and market conditions.

The problem with established companies that have lost market share is that when implementing a new business strategy, they focus on the "how"; that is, they analyze alternatives on how to reduce or improve what they are currently managing operationally. Generally, they concentrate their efforts on the following activities:

- Organizational restructuring, activities, and production, among others.
- Process and activity reengineering.
- Quality control.
- Cost strategy.

However, they leave out the "who" and "what" aspects, failing to consider or evaluate the change that consumers are undergoing, the needs they demand to cover, and their current requirements.

The intention is to discover a unique strategic position that helps us become more competitive in the market by creating value for our customers and investors, not a cost reduction that allows us to be profitable in the short term. We say this because once the cost reduction is realized, other competitors may begin to replicate the same practice, so this strategy will only serve us until the market adjusts. In contrast, when we exhibit a unique strategic position, other competitors take longer to copy our activities, and this way, we gain a competitive advantage over the others.

3.2 Creating a Strategic Plan

The first thing advised is to define who will create the company's strategic plan. The company leaders should prepare it to be effective, not only because they will execute it but also because they know the organization's qualities and the business environment. If they don't identify with it, its execution won't be 100% effective. The initial commitment to change the strategy and make it practical involves frontline leaders feeling committed.

In addition to these leaders, the work team can participate as support for collecting data and information about customer behavior and the market since they are the ones who interact the most with them and know their needs. A strategic plan that doesn't start from precise information about the sector, customers, and market positioning, relying solely on leaders' recommendations, won't be 100% effective either. The team comprises people who interact daily with customer demands, remembering that to add value, we need to add new ingredients that enhance the consumer experience.

From this perspective, an excellent strategic plan answers the following questions:
1. What is the assessment of the market analysis?
2. How well does it analyze existing markets and customer needs?
3. What is the best way to motivate profitable business growth, and what are the obstacles to progress?
4. Who are our competitors?
5. Does the business have the capability to execute the strategy?
6. Are short and long-term objectives aligned?
7. What are the critical goals of plan execution?
8. What are the most relevant challenges the business faces?

Likewise, the two most important questions must be answered: How will we sustainably make money with this new strategy? And what opportunity cost does it represent for the business and investors? Having a good level of detail in these answers is crucial, as they determine whether investors or shareholders will support us.

This analysis is fundamental for any operation we plan to undertake. If we can't understand how we will make money with the proposed plan in five minutes, it means that the project is too complex and needs to be redesigned to generate benefits for the organization.

The creation of the strategy follows a chronological model that we must adhere to implement efficiently in our companies or businesses. These steps must be taken meticulously because if proper diligence is not exercised in one of them, the desired effect of the subsequent steps will not be achieved. The steps we will aim to cover are:

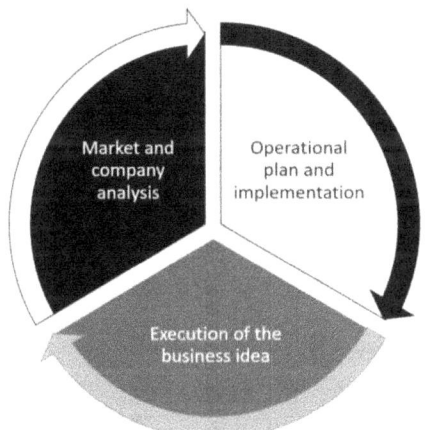

These activities provide us with a guide on where to begin our business strategic plan. They allow us to identify each of the events we must address for implementation and gain a competitive advantage over our competitors, adding value to customer service and the performance of shareholders and investors.

When materializing the strategic position, we need to envision ourselves as the shareholders or investors of our business, whether we're starting from scratch or have been working on it for some time. We should also seek internal collaborators to help enrich it (in the case of an ongoing business), relying on those individuals who have a deeper understanding of the operations and have witnessed the evolution of our company.

In any case, it's not recommended to develop the business idea alone; it's always good to have a different perspective than our own about our company and where we want to go.

3.3 Market and Company Analysis

With the proper analysis of the market and the company, the following questions from the strategic plan are answered:
1. What is the evaluation of the market analysis?
2. How well does it analyze existing markets and customer needs?
3. Who are our competitors?
4. Does the business have the capability to execute the strategy?

The first evaluation to complete is the SWOT analysis of the business (Strengths, Weaknesses, Opportunities, and Threats) to recognize where we stand. This way, we conduct a comprehensive analysis of the industry, the environment, and the company to identify our strengths and weaknesses, as well as to understand the opportunities and threats in the sector or market we are in.

The environmental analysis encompasses all the factors that exist and are constantly changing in the sector where we are established. It involves examining each of the components, such as sociocultural, technological, political, and economic factors, and within these, detecting the opportunities we need to capitalize on and evaluating the future threats the business will face.

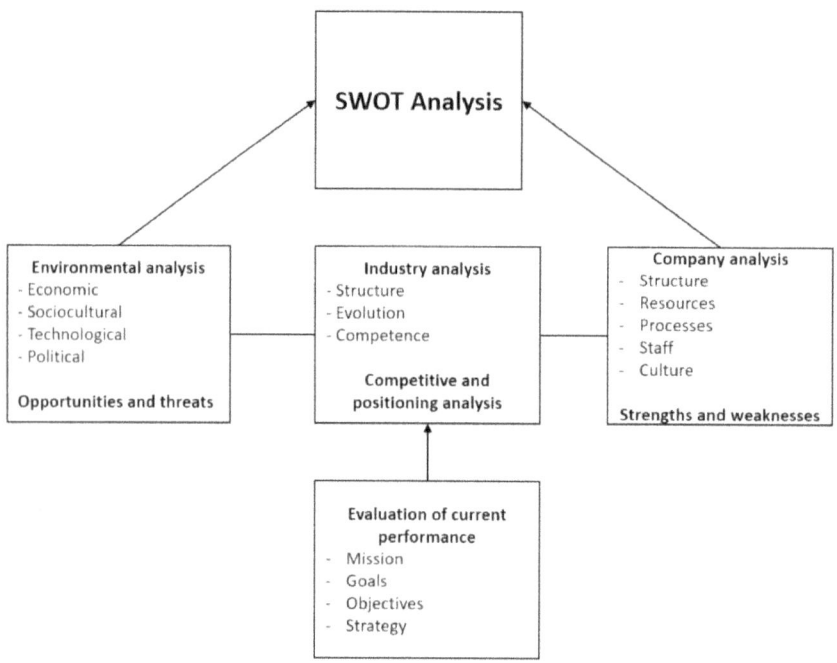

Now, we analyze the current situation, trends, and future changes that will arise in our environment, the potential alliances of competitors, the new regulations (or deregulations) the market will undergo new technologies, and consumer trends.

This provides us with a framework for understanding our business's environment, what we are capitalizing on from what currently exists, and how we will deal with the new developments our sector will undergo. On the other hand, considering the surrounding environment tells us where to act and what needs to be included in our strategy to make a difference.

The environmental analysis helps us become aware of the needs and behaviors of our current and potential customers. A common mistake businesses make when developing a strategic plan is that they focus it internally, meaning they are primarily based on how to manufacture and sell their products or services rather than finding out what the market demands and how it demands it. In this regard, conducting consumer satisfaction surveys to study trends, preferences, and tastes is crucial, as producing a product nobody requires will ultimately shift us from our current position to an ineffective one.

The key to understanding these factors is clearly pinpointing the business idea's market. Sometimes, the problem lies in misidentifying the market; consequently, we need to understand our consumers' behavior and decision-making process.

Let's take an example: if we were manufacturers of pens and wanted to increase the profitability of the business, we should clearly and objectively specify our market: i) consumers who purchase a pen for personal use, ii) consumers who buy a pen to gift to someone else; iii) companies that use pens to imprint their brand for promotional purposes; and iv) companies that acquire pens to give as gifts to their customers.

The quality a customer requires in a pen for gifting to someone they value and the demands of a company that needs pens to give to their most distinguished customers differ from those who buy it for personal use or in bulk for promotional activities. If the market is poorly defined, everything we do won't achieve the desired purpose.

Deciphering the industry helps us accurately determine who interacts in the market where we have a presence: how the market is composed, who our competitors are, and how the market has evolved since its inception.

When analyzing the competition, it's not only about naming them but also delving into the analysis by evaluating their structure, the composition of their executive team, how they make decisions, what decisions they would make if we applied our strategy, what sets us apart from them, and what we can use to our advantage.

It's suggested to avoid limiting the analysis of the competition to merely listing them as if they were in a phone book. The purpose of identifying our direct competitors is to assess which actions to consider in response to a change in our current strategy. Furthermore, it's advisable to study each of the competitors in the market we'll face and have the appropriate tools for reactions upon entering the market.

Depending on the market, different variables of each competitor need to be examined as to how much they influence the customer segment. The main goal is to cover the following:

- Understand the market share of each participant in the market.
- Decrypt the annual revenues of competitors and the projection they estimate for the upcoming period.
- Evaluate the new market share distribution with our inclusion in the sector.
- Validate the products or services of the competition and understand why consumers choose them.
- Inquire about the competitors' responsiveness to changes in the market.
- Analyze how active competitors are in the target market segment.
- Inspect which competitors are innovative, which differentiate themselves, which are lagging, and which are more reserved.
- Detail the techniques used by competitors to market their products:
    - ✓ Pricing.
    - ✓ Number of establishments.
    - ✓ Customer service.
    - ✓ Organizational distribution.
    - ✓ Communication channels.
    - ✓ Promotions.

The aim is to identify, analyze, and evaluate their strengths and weaknesses, thereby exploring our opportunities in that market segment and determining the threats we will face (if any).

Here's a comparative table model to examine the most significant variables of a sector:

Variables	Company A	Company B	Company C	Company D
Brand Presence	1	4	5	3
Prices	3	3	4	5
Communication Channels	1	5	5	4
Product/Service Quality	3	4	4	5
Customer Service	3	4	4	5
Market Share	2	4	5	4
Distribution Channels	2	5	4	3
Number of Establishments	2	5	5	3

The proposal is to use a Likert-type scale, with a scoring range from 1 to 5, to confirm whether competitors' participation is high or low:
- Very Low = 1
- Low = 2
- Neutral = 3
- High = 4
- Very High = 5

This way, we have a more comprehensive understanding of the competitors and how they interact in the market, providing us with more detailed information for decision-making and handling competitor reactions.

For example, we decided to lower the prices of our pen factory's products to make them more attractive to companies looking to include their brand and run promotions. In that case, we should consider how other competitors would react. If one or all of them lowered their prices as well, we wouldn't have the "supposed attractiveness," and perhaps due to their cost structure, the competition would achieve higher returns than us by reducing their price. In conclusion, we would diminish the company's current profits while maintaining the same market share. Therefore, it's crucial to analyze competitors and their actions to assess and mitigate risks.

On the other hand, reviewing how the market has evolved is valuable because each sector has responded differently over the years, with some experiencing more rapid changes than others. An example of this is the mobile phone manufacturing sector. Every six months, the technology of the devices changes, so the industry has a faster evolutionary trend than sectors like pen manufacturing. However, there's always evolution. If we analyze the pen sector, we will notice that current consumer tastes and preferences are very different from those of the 1990s.

Based on what's been said, it's suggested that we evaluate our behavior concerning the market and competitors, conducting an internal analysis of how our constituent components align with the market we're targeting. Therefore, this means assessing how our vision, mission, and values align with the current strategy and how we'll apply these elements to our new strategy.

We should ask ourselves: Does the new strategy appropriately apply to our constituent elements? Are these constituent elements correct? Do we need to make changes to our constituent elements? Are our vision and mission in line with current markets? How does the current strategy respond to market demands? Are my current objectives aligned with the current strategy? These answers are advisable to have clear, as they determine the successful execution of the strategic plan as the core of the business or as the reason for its existence, in other words, the philosophy of the stakeholders.

Similarly, to complete our SWOT analysis, we must understand our company and observe how it's structured in terms of resources, processes, personnel, culture, and other internal variables. We must remember that a strategic position must consider whether it can be executed with our resources.

Sometimes, we create a strategic plan without considering that our current staff might need the necessary skills to carry it out. Interpreting the above, if our pen factory was focused on mass consumption and the new direction was to produce pens with the highest market standards, we would need to assess the training of our sales force or expand it to sell this new product line.

In conclusion, the SWOT analysis will yield the following conclusions about the sector where our business operations are:

Potential Internal Strengths

- Optimal financial structure.
- Excellent positioning among buyers.
- Market visibility.
- Strategic functional areas.
- Possibility of economies of scale.
- Reduced intense competitive pressures.
- Accepted advertising campaigns.
- Innovation skills.
- Proven management skills.
- Marked experience curve.
- High capacity for product or technology manufacturing.
- Advanced technological techniques.

Potential External Opportunities

- Expansion opportunity to new markets or customer segments.
- Mechanisms to expand the product line to cover a wider variety of customer needs.
- Ability to transfer knowledge from new business lines or new production processes.
- Deepening the value chain forward and backward.
- Opening to attractive foreign markets.
- Growth opportunity due to niche availability in emerging markets.
- Emergence of new technologies.

Potential Internal Weaknesses

- Unclear strategic vision.
- Outdated facilities.
- Poor profitability.
- Weaknesses in human resources and business leaders.
- Lack of critical skills or techniques for the targeted market.
- Poor implementation track record.
- Internal operational deficiencies.
- Lack of forward-looking research and development.
- Low product diversification.
- Market impact of the weak image.
- Weak supply chain.
- Below-market promotion tools.
- Inability to bear the financial costs of business strategic changes.
- High unit costs compared to competitors.

Potential External Threats

- Opening of the market to foreign competitors with better cost distribution.
- Increase in demand for substitute products.
- Market expansion levels stagnation.
- Excessive increase in foreign currency exchange rates and trade policies.
- High investment to meet required standards and obligations.
- Inability to cope with different economic cycles.
- Variability in consumer tastes and preferences.
- External conditions negatively impact, causing demographic variations.

Each of these elements is essential for a sectoral analysis of the environment in which we operate or where we intend to drive our business. We must be meticulous when considering each factor, as creating false hopes or making promises about uncertain factors is not recommended. This ultimately reflects on our business idea, exposing us to each of the variables we didn't consider in the analysis.

We must be aware that the easy path leads to a long and challenging journey, while the rugged and narrow path leads us straight to a more comfortable route. All of this is subsequently reflected in the results of our efforts in forging a business with the necessary criteria to achieve the expected outcomes.

The provided information yields the following graph of the environmental analysis:

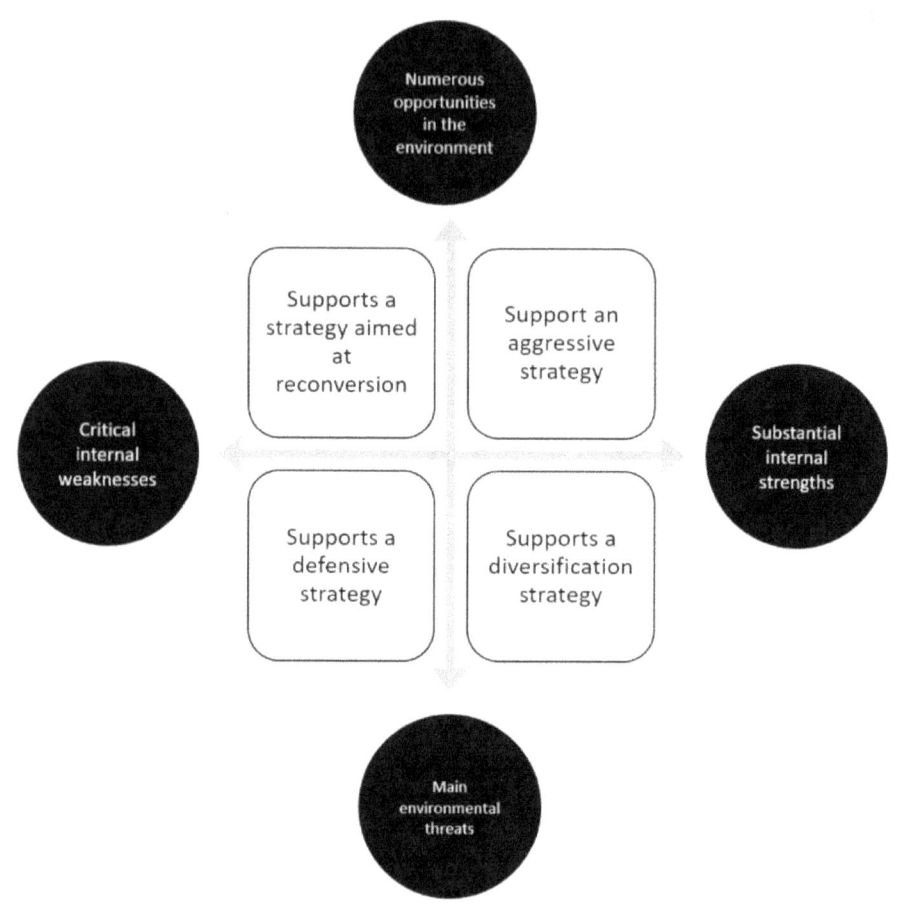

3.3.1 Porter's Five Forces

We can incorporate Porter's competitive forces into our environmental analysis as they explore industry dependencies based on five forces: the threat of new entrants, the bargaining power of customers, the bargaining power of suppliers, the threat of substitute products or services, and the rivalry among existing competitors.

Porter emphasizes the need to identify how influential the different rivals are in the market where we operate, analyzing each of them effectively. This rivalry is explained by Porter as follows[6]:

a) Entry barriers to the industry. It refers to current market participants' advantage over those trying to enter the industry. These are the threats faced by new entrants:
- ✓ *Capital is required for entry.* This is often observed in companies that require significant infrastructure and machinery purchases to start operations. High capital requirements can also relate to inventory supply to meet consumer needs, costs associated with offering credit to customers, advertising, research and development, and estimating the losses incurred when starting a new business.
- ✓ *Customer lock-in or product differentiation.* This refers to adjustments made by market participants for their customers, such as software installations for order processing or product adaptations for personalization. In the case of product adaptations, the cost for a customer to switch to a different provider is so high that it becomes nearly impossible to change, which is common in highly specialized industries like aerospace or shipbuilding.
- ✓ *Distribution channels.* Product distribution depends on production volume and the market penetration of competitors. If production volume is low and competitors have a high market penetration, they will have better distribution channels than new market entrants, creating inequality.
- ✓ *Government regulations.* Entry into a particular market depends on government regulations.
- ✓ *Cost disadvantages.* Some market participants can enjoy cost advantages regardless of their size. This often occurs due to patents they hold, their access to technology, higher process efficiency,

---

[6] Porter, M.E. (2009). To be competitive. Boston: Harvard Business Press.

access to raw materials, or specific geographical regions, among other factors.
- ✓ *Economies of scale from both supply and demand.* Supply-side economies of scale refer to lower unit costs as production volume increases, resulting in more attractive consumer prices. Demand-side economies of scale occur when suppliers lower prices as buyers raise orders, preventing smaller companies from entering.

b) Bargaining power of suppliers. It depends on the number of suppliers in the industry we're entering and how specialized our product is. If there are only a few suppliers of raw materials in our market, they can exert influence by limiting quantities, raising prices, and other behaviors. Their influence is high when:
- ✓ Few suppliers exist in the industry.
- ✓ Suppliers are not dependent on a single market.
- ✓ Raw materials are specialized and hard to replace.
- ✓ Industry participants have specialized operations through software installations, product adaptations, etc.
- ✓ New entrants are not attractive to suppliers.
- ✓ Supplier products are patented, and brand quality or influence is prominent in the sector (e.g., pharmaceuticals with patented medications).
- ✓ Suppliers can threaten industry participants by being attracted to their profit margins and deciding to enter the industry, potentially displacing some of their clients.

c) Bargaining power of customers. This occurs when our customers influence negotiating the products they consume, affecting our profitability. Customers often exert influence in the following cases:
- ✓ A limited customer base.
- ✓ Products are generic or have little differentiation from other market options, encouraging customers to choose any option.

- ✓ Price variations are minimal, giving consumers the choice of purchase.
- ✓ The number of buyers in the industry exerts influence, as a few can significantly impact the market.
- ✓ Low investment costs for changing suppliers make switching easy.
- ✓ Buyers have a substantial impact on sales.
- ✓ Buyers can threaten suppliers by attempting backward integration, meaning if we are distributors of rice bags, we can integrate backward by opening a rice mill.

d) Rivalry among existing competitors. How participants in a market compete determines the profits or benefits achievable in that industry. It's essential to know who the different participants are to understand the rivalry in the sector, which is driven by intensity or the underlying bases.

Intensity can occur in the following cases:
- ✓ When there are many competitors in the same market or if structures and market share are similar.
- ✓ In a mature industry with slow progress, participants aim to capture market share from others.
- ✓ Exiting the market is difficult for companies due to high investments or current commitments.
- ✓ Participants' aspirations to advance in the market, their commitment to the company, or their driving ideology.

As for rivalry based on underlying bases can arise from complementary services, delivery times, brand potential, product benefits, or price. If competitors focus on price, consumers may ignore what they can receive or the quality of products but rather on economic savings. This type of rivalry occurs when:

- ✓ Products offered by competitors are standardized, generic, or have minimal differentiation.

- ✓ Economies of scale exist among participants, leading to excess production to sustain low prices and capture more market share.
- ✓ Products have a limited lifespan or are subject to obsolescence, prompting price reductions to sell them before their value diminishes (common in the technology and perishable goods industries).

e) Substitute products. These are items that customers consume outside of what we offer. They don't necessarily have to be similar but serve the same function or purpose in some way. Examples include emails as substitutes for courier-delivered letters or video game consoles as substitutes for amusement parks. Both options yield the same result: in the first case, they're similar and serve the same function; in the second case, they're different but hold the same meaning for users.

As substitutes become more influential in our industry, participants' profitability decreases, limiting price flexibility. A high concentration of substitutes in the industry occurs when:
- ✓ Substitutes' costs are low compared to industry products.
- ✓ The substitute product's offering significantly impacts the market at a relatively similar price to the industries.

It's crucial to consider all these factors for the new plan, evaluating our current status to leverage strengths and improve weaknesses. These factors also indicate how we're positioned against direct competitors and how to use this positioning to our advantage. This way, we can make processes more efficient, enhance our structure, identify necessary additional procedures, and understand the current business environment.

A competent analysis provides robust information for business leaders, making decision-making easier when all involved variables are managed. It's also essential to be aware of which activities we excel in and which we don't, as confusion can arise during the implementation of new business lines. We might have production capacity but need to gain experience in production or knowledge of the market. For instance, if we have space in the pen factory to produce thermometers but lack qualified personnel for production or information on the market, experience, or sales staff for the new product, production won't yield the desired results and could even impact the current market position of pens.

3.4 Internal Company Analysis

Just as we analyze the market and competition, we must perform an internal analysis of our business (current or future), create a comprehensive structure to visualize strengths and weaknesses and evaluate which activities add value to our products or services.

The value chain focuses on two primary activities:

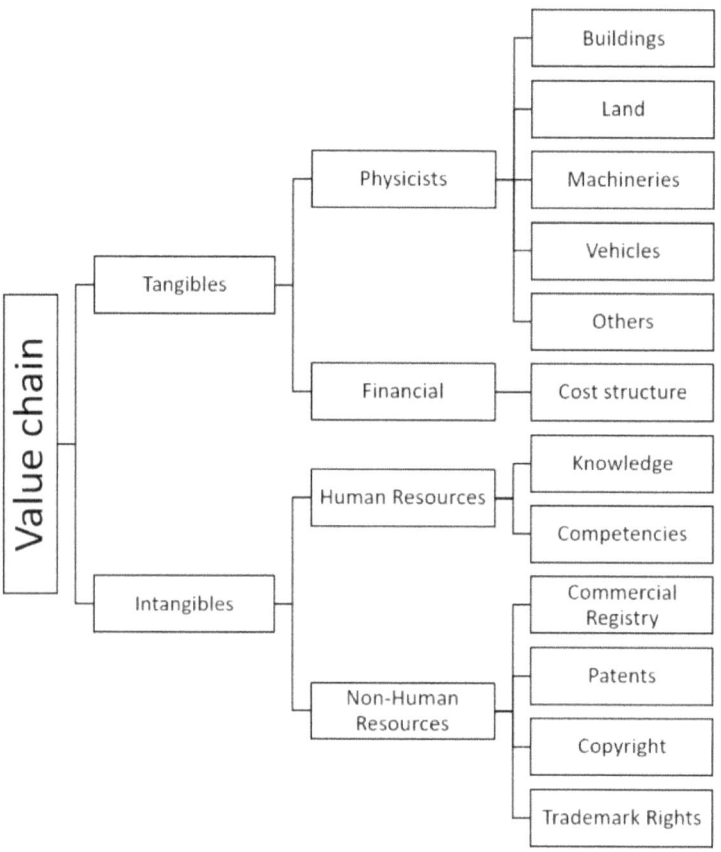

After we have defined our value chain, which is to say, the activities that add value to the service or product we offer, we must prepare a comparative analysis or benchmarking of the competition to decipher our strengths and weaknesses in which areas. The study requires us to be very honest and accurately work with these qualities.

The comparative analysis is conducted by contrasting our structure with each of our direct and potential competitors to understand precisely what we are facing in all aspects. This practice is widespread among companies to assess their appearance compared to competitors.

It should be clarified that this is not an espionage practice or about copying the competition. It is simply about identifying strengths and weaknesses. For this reason, it is recommended to dedicate an appropriate amount of time to the study to research and learn about where we stand in the sector we are interacting with or planning to interact with.

With our benchmarking, we will not measure all the activities we perform but only those critical activities that are essential for providing the service or product. These activities will provide us with the value chain.

3.5 Company Diagnosis

After identifying strengths, opportunities, weaknesses, and threats, we must carry out a diagnosis of the situation at hand and develop a strategic plan. There's no point in mastering various factors if we don't have an action plan that helps us improve our competitive position.

In the following image, we counterbalance the SWOT analysis with an action measure for each of the variables:

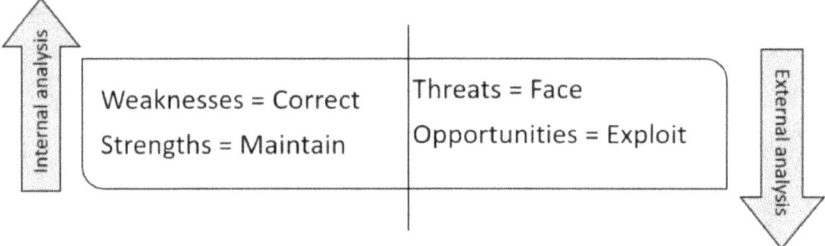

Based on the internal and external analysis of the business, this graph allows us to analyze each of the variables we have seen in our SWOT analysis so that we can extract an effective action plan to act in each situation.

CHAPTER IV: OPERATIONAL PLAN AND IMPLEMENTATION

After addressing the market analysis and the environment in which we participate, it is recommended that we add the following two questions to our strategic plan: Where should we go? How do we get there?

These points are critical in our business strategy, as they will guide us when executing it and indicate how to leverage our resources. This means we must evaluate our business units and the entire company to devise strategic options and verify each, observing their implications regarding resource requirements, opportunity costs, and return on investment.

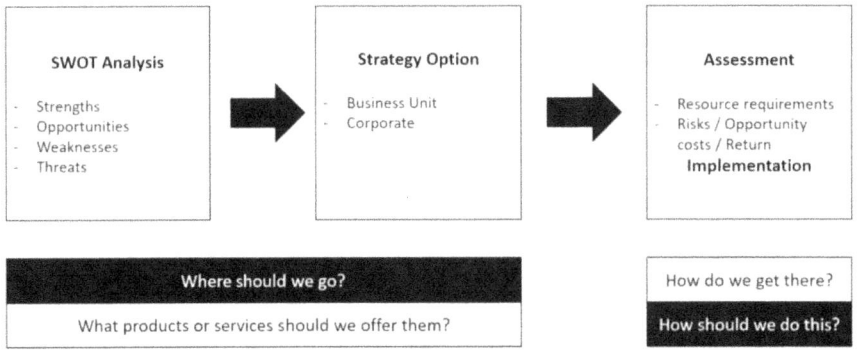

At this point, we will answer the following questions:
1. What is the best way to make the business grow profitably, and what obstacles exist to progress?
2. Are short-term and long-term objectives aligned?
3. What are the main execution goals?
4. What are the most relevant challenges that the business faces?

When examining different ways to motivate profitable business growth and identifying obstacles, we must review the entire company's structure, each business unit, policies, culture, and philosophy.

Many companies are not usually innovative for the following reasons:
- ✓ *Internal politics:* Employees are accustomed to performing activities the same way they always have and firmly adhere to internal business policies, affecting their ability to understand things beyond the current framework.
- ✓ *Self-satisfaction:* Many companies are in their comfort zone and do not consider the possibility of continuing to grow due to a lack of competitors. Often, a new competitor enters the market and takes away a significant portion of their market share.
- ✓ *Fear of cannibalizing existing product lines:* Companies sometimes cling to the current market without considering its evolution, which leaves them behind.
- ✓ *General lack of incentives to give up a secure present for an uncertain future:* Some companies fail to see the "big picture" clearly and lack the motivation to see how it unfolds.

It's advised to understand that a business strategy is not written in stone and lasts centuries; instead, it presents where we will focus over five years. As mentioned, the world is rapidly changing, and if we adapt, we'll be included in the market.

To be effective, it's recommended that we review our strategy annually and make adjustments as market changes arise. We should develop a three-year strategy that allows us to establish a concrete position and then check it repeatedly. Many make the mistake of having a plan so long that by the time they take their first steps, the market no longer exists, like when they started their businesses.

It's essential to answer the following questions in this part of the strategic plan to understand how to move forward and what obstacles are present:
- Does the business need to create new products or new distribution channels?

- Is there a need to attract new customers or better leverage existing ones?
- Is it better to venture into other businesses or continue progressing in the current one?
- Can costs be cut without affecting the quality of the current product or manufactured at a lower cost?

It's important to clarify that these questions are not exclusive; in other words, a business might need new products and new distribution channels because the current ones do not meet market needs. It's also possible that the business benefits from existing customers but still need to tap into a new market niche. We must answer these questions assertively based on the SWOT analysis we conducted earlier.

In this regard, we must draw on the SWOT analysis for various reasons. If we understand that the business needs a cost reduction without compromising quality, but such action might trigger a response from the competition, the dominant competitor (if it's not us) might have a more significant profit margin, allowing them to reduce costs more efficiently and nullify our actions.

We also recommend determining whether short-term objectives are intrinsically aligned with long-term objectives. By this, we mean whether short-term investments or changes align with what we intend to achieve in the long term.

We can provide an example based on a pen manufacturing factory. If we consider the possibility of entering the high-end pen market to offer exclusive and elegant gifts, and for this, we need to invest in expanding current facilities for a specialized new machine and allocate funds for a new location that meets consumer demands, we need to evaluate whether these short-term investments will yield the returns and positioning we expect in five years (long-term goal). It's only possible to acquire a new position if, in the end, the latest market will yield the expected returns. Therefore, we need to verify short-term objectives to ensure they deliver the necessary long-term results and avoid investing in strategies that won't be profitable for the business.

Every business idea comes with strategies or objectives that must be fulfilled, and the ability to manage them makes the idea more realistic and adaptable to market changes. If we don't choose the most essential strategies to build the concept, execution becomes nearly impossible.

On the other hand, it's suggested that we understand the most relevant factors that affect our business to effectively devise a way to act to improve our current position. Competent competitors undertake this analysis to formulate their strategies. These factors can be seen as the "Achilles' heel" that needs protection.

The answer every investor requires is how the business will make money sustainably with the strategy and what opportunity cost it represents. In this regard, we need to consider the following questions to identify how we'll generate income:

- Is the customer willing to pay an extra premium in the price for the changes we're making?
- Do we have what it takes to be efficient in this new market?
- How are costs and cost distribution affected in the short and long term?
- What is the investment cost?
- Will there be only an initial investment, or will investments be required at different periods?

These fundamental questions should be answered regarding profits, as shareholders and investors will numerically measure the return the business strategy will yield.

Furthermore, we need to answer impact-related questions in terms of the opportunity cost the business strategy represents for shareholders, investors, and the company:

- How much-working capital does the new business idea require?
- What actions must be implemented to move forward with the new strategic plan?
- What is the investment required to market the new product?

Considering the opportunity cost we described earlier, these questions need to be analyzed, i.e., what we are giving up to develop the new business strategic plan and what this new idea represents compared to our current position. Engaging in these exercises is crucial to objectively identify the changes we're making and what we expect from them.

The most common questions and objections we encounter from shareholders and investors are as follows:

- **Question:** Why abandon what we're doing to risk something uncertain?
  Reasoning: The investor thinks along these lines: "Currently, we have an established business that yields a significant annual return compared to the rest of the market, and we have a slight improvement in sales. So why change strategy if the current one has worked for us?"

- **Question:** What will we invest in?
  Reasoning: We often find mental paradigms among shareholders because most companies were founded in the likeness of their founders, and everything is based on this model. As a result, they maintain "sacred cows" that prevent them from thinking beyond their current state.

- **Question:** How can we be sure the strategy will be effective?
  Reasoning: Even when the new business idea is effectively communicated, investors will question whether it's truly the best option or why they should change the current position for an uncertain one with unknown outcomes.

- **Question:** Can the strategy be carried out with the current business position?
  Reasoning: If investors are convinced that this new business strategy has the potential to be beneficial for the company, the next question would be whether both operations can be conducted concurrently. This is because they are deeply attached to their current position and fear change.

As we'll always encounter concerns from shareholders and investors, we must decipher the fundamental aspects to change their mindset and present the new strategic position straightforwardly. These aspects include:

1. Defining the target market for the business, consumer trends, and the current business pattern.
2. Identifying whom to attract as customers, what products or services to offer them, and how to develop the new business scheme.
3. We are creating an organizational environment centered around the new strategic plan.

Remember that we can prepare all existing market studies and analyses, but if we don't know how to address the mental frameworks of business shareholders and investors, we won't be able to establish a new strategic position. Furthermore, we're shaping a business idea for a new venture and seeking investment from investors. In that case, addressing the previously described questions about how the idea will generate income is essential. For them, what matters most is how profitable it is. The presentation should be simple and straightforward, without excessive complications, as otherwise, it's understood that the answer isn't well understood.

4.1 Canvas Model

We support our analysis by completing the Value Creation Canvas, as it provides us with a 360-degree view of the business. This system is effective because it's easy to understand and visualize the differentiators of our business, whether it's new or already operational. The goal is to guide our strategy towards creating a more competitive presence in the market.

The framework starts with a description of the following aspects:

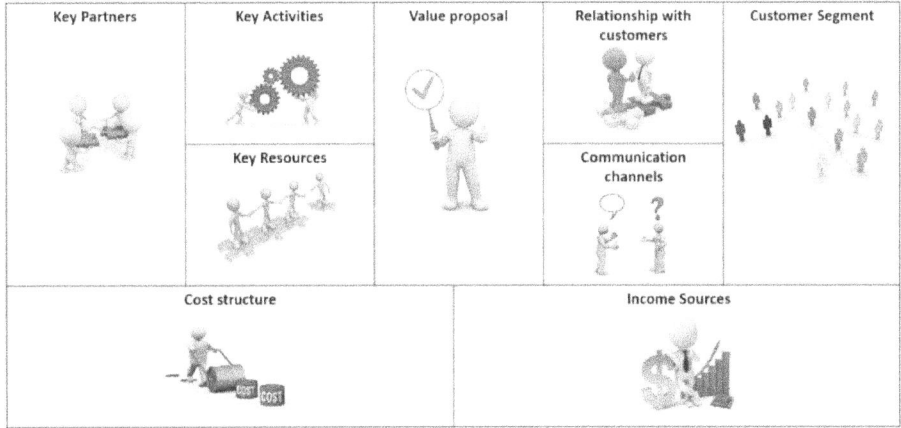

4.1.1 Key Partners

Refers to selecting suitable suppliers for our business and managing good relationships with partners for mutual collaborations. In any case, it will depend on what we pursue, such as finding key profiles (partners), selecting suppliers, merging companies, etc.

Returning to the mass-produced pen factory example, we want to adopt a more competitive strategic position where we enhance customer satisfaction. To achieve this, we will merge with a company that specializes in high-end pens. They will provide the manufacturing, distribution, and marketing structure while we supply working capital. They will return a portion of the net profits to us as compensation. This move will expand our business line and lead to a new market share position.

4.1.2 Key Activities

These internal activities within the company are essential to deliver what customers expect, translating into revenue. These tasks characterize the business we are conducting, i.e., what we must do to offer the product or service we provide. For instance, these tasks can include distribution, transportation, and advertising, among other necessary activities to run the business. The critical activity is pen production if we put it into practice in our pen factory.

All activities related to pen production are fundamental to our company. Others are not considered vital, as the essence of our business is pen production. In other words, the Canvas model defines "key activities" only as those directly related to the core business. This is where we need to focus our attention, as these activities generate income for the company.

4.1.3 Key Resources

These are the foundations on which our business relies, encompassing internal actions that ensure the efficient management of economic activities. These pillars uphold our company and that we need to rely on to develop our trade. This includes physical resources (machinery, computers, facilities, communication equipment, etc.), intellectual resources (databases and programs), economic resources (funds needed to cover physical and variable expenses), and human resources for operations management.

In the pen factory, some of our essential resources are the machinery and technology for pen production. Another vital resource is the technicians and engineers operating the production plants.

4.1.4 Market Segment or Customers

This aims to define whom we are targeting and who the actual customers are—the decision-makers purchasing the products. Additionally, it helps identify the market niche we are focusing on, allowing the company's activities to cater to these consumers. The effectiveness of our efforts depends on an accurate market description.

To define the customer segment, we assess whether this audience is financially attractive for the business. Many companies identify their ideal customers, but different customers consume their products. Specifying a market niche we wish to attract would be counterproductive when our products are intended for a completely different market segment. Hence, we must identify the product consumers, decision-makers, and their decision-making processes. We should verify if these are the appropriate customers or if we need to redesign the approach because our product or service doesn't align with the described market segment.

In our mass-produced pen factory, we might incorrectly identify gift-givers as the target audience. This misalignment means no matter how much effort we put into the strategy, we won't meet the customer's expectations, as they require a different, higher-end product.

The practical approach would be to focus our efforts on prominent corporations' marketing or advertising executives who acquire pens for their brand promotions (a more suitable customer segment for our company). It's important to note that we haven't defined large corporations as the market segment but rather as the decision-makers who purchase our product. This leads to a more practical direction.

When defining our customers, caution is crucial, as it determines the competence of the strategic position. In this regard, there are three ways to specify the target market: (1) by-product, (2) by-product functionality, and (3) by customer's basic needs.

In the high-end pen factory: (1) by-product, it's the pen sales business; (2) by functionality, it's the communication business as it's a tool for communication; and (3) by basic needs, it's the status-enhancing business due to the cost of the pens, making the product accessible to only specific individuals.

Customer segmentation is also helpful in visualizing existing potential businesses, analyzing the competition, discovering specific market needs for adjusting the offer, and establishing priorities when entering the sector.

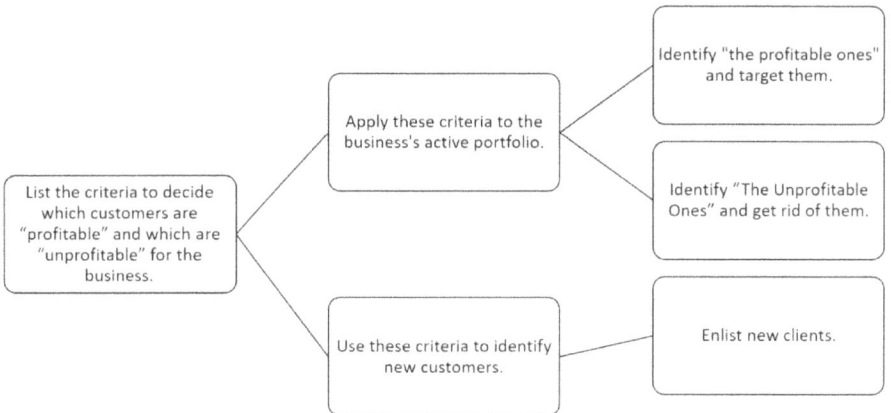

Certain criteria need to be considered when choosing a specific market segment:

- We intend to target the growth of the sector.
- The size of the market niche we will capture.
- The future projection of the market segment.
- We wish to target the differentiation from current products in the market.

If we haven't yet defined our target customer or the market we will focus on; we need to find out whom to target as customers and what to offer them. This will shed light when starting a new business or shifting customer segments. Many perform this analysis and target the wrong customer segment, causing the business idea to be ineffective.

We can create a framework to identify which customers are profitable for our business and which are not. This framework helps us determine which customers will provide the desired income for our business without harming our current market position. Simultaneously, we discard those that do not align with our purposes and are not profitable enough for our company. This approach allows us to list the activities to be carried out efficiently.

It's essential to ensure that our business idea aligns with the latent needs of a specific market segment, which is advised to be well-defined. We must focus on what consumers demand and how to meet the current market's unfulfilled needs so we avoid falling into the trap of having an attractive idea that fails to meet consumers' minimum expectations.

4.1.5 Customer Relationships

This point is crucial as it outlines how we will build customer loyalty and what type of relationships we will have with them—whether we will have personalized contact or if customers will self-serve. We need to specify what impact our brand will have on customers. We concretely examine how our company will manage relationships with the target audience. For this purpose, we observe the characteristics of consumers within the sector, thus defining the customer relationship that strengthens the value chain and standardizes service.

In the mass-produced pen factory, we can offer a personalized service by visiting direct consumers (marketing executives of prominent corporations) to present the product proposition and identify their needs. The product is used to promote these customers' brands, creating a positive effect as we personalize the service and guide them in their selection.

We could have employed a self-service system where consumers access a website, select the pen type they desire, specify the quantity, make payment, and we deliver the product to their address. However, we observed that our customer segment prefers personalized contact with a business executive who presents the product portfolio. This is why we adopted the customized approach to customer interaction.

This determines how we establish relationships with customers in the business. Adopting a relationship model now and later introducing other relationship patterns with the same customers isn't advisable, as it won't contribute to meeting their expectations. Initially, it's recommended to decode consumer behavior to understand the best way to serve them and establish it as part of our policies.

4.1.6 Communication Channels

Communication channels aim to deliver messages about the products or services we provide to our customers. This involves specifying how we reach our critical consumers and establishing the most effective means to communicate with them. To do this, we consider the following:
- ✓ The environment of our customers.
- ✓ What are they exposed to?
- ✓ Which mediums have the most influence on them?
- ✓ What kind of offers are they exposed to?
- ✓ The products they consume and how they obtain them.

One option in our pen factory might be to use magazines as a communication channel. We could showcase new prototypes with their respective features and a catalog of available models, targeting corporate marketing executives to showcase the product.

4.1.7 Cost Structure

The economic model explains that we must thoroughly study our costs, which allows us to identify areas needing more attention and address them appropriately to enhance efficiency. Every business has a different cost distribution, making it essential to scrutinize them to prevent improper management from absorbing the revenue. It's imperative to explore the main costs of the business (fixed costs and predictable variable costs) and the activities that incur the most expenses. By managing these costs effectively, we can add value to the company and increase revenue.

In our pen factory, the cost structure would be based on three pillars: personnel, fixed costs, and costs related to technological advancements for process efficiency.

4.1.8 Revenue Streams

We analyze how customers acquire products, what they desire, and what they are willing to pay for them. Additionally, we assess different revenue sources in our business that might still need to be fully explored and how to create new revenue streams based on existing activities.

As a guide, consider:
- ✓ How much are customers willing to pay?
- ✓ How frequently do our consumers make purchases?
- ✓ What quantities do our consumers buy?
- ✓ Where do our customers sell the products? (if our customers are resellers)
- ✓ How do customers pay for services?
- ✓ What are the additional revenue sources in our business aren't an integral part of our core activity?

This helps make a sound decision about how to provide the service or present the product, ensuring we offer customers what they expect based on what they are paying or willing to pay.

4.1.9 Value Proposition

This refers to the product or service we offer the public, allowing us to retain and expand our customer base by providing the best value for their money. Here, we detail the features that make our product or service unique.

To outline this proposition, we suggest considering the following inquiries:
- ✓ What do customers expect to receive?
- ✓ What kind of relationship are they willing to establish?
- ✓ What are their concerns?
- ✓ What truly matters to them?
- ✓ What problems do they currently encounter with the services or products they consume?
- ✓ What is their attitude toward this?
- ✓ What motivates them?
- ✓ What do they truly need or want to achieve?

Suppose we don't understand our customers and their needs. In that case, we might end up offering a product or service that already exists in the market or a product or service that doesn't fulfill consumers' requirements.

Adding value through our services or products is the essence of our business as we establish a company to meet current or future consumer needs. Therefore, it's recommended to be open to listening to customer feedback to enhance the products or services we provide. Most complaints or comments are expressed because customers want to remain loyal and avoid turning to the competition.

CHAPTER V: BUSINESS IDEA REVIEW

After designing our business idea, confirming that it aligns well with reality is prudent. Furthermore, this entails reviewing all points comprehensively and ensuring we understand all the plan's variables. This review analyzes the business idea from different perspectives, considering each company department: finance, business, human resources, public relations, marketing, advertising, etc.

We strive to ensure that each area is adequately covered by formulating questions that address new concerns:
- ✓ Do different business units deeply understand our competition and their capabilities?
- ✓ Does our organization have the capability to execute the business idea?
- ✓ Has the business idea been effectively communicated with our workforce and their interaction?
- ✓ Are these ideas appropriate?

We aim to ensure that different factors involved in implementing the new idea are considered, measure market reactions, and verify how the strategy aligns with reality.

If the business unit isn't fully aware of our competition's capabilities, we might be vulnerable to their reactions. Hence, it's essential to consider their potential moves to anticipate them. Therefore, we propose answering the following questions:
- ✓ How does our competition manage the customer segment we aim to capture, and what prevents other competitors from reducing their market share?
- ✓ What do we know about the business structure of our competitors? (Emphasizing their training, market know-how, and whether it's suitable for serving the market)
- ✓ What strategies do our competitors use to gain more market share?

- ✓ How will they react to our market entry with our business idea?
- ✓ Are they joining forces, or is one competitor absorbing another to consolidate its position and gain more market share?

Many business ideas are developed without considering whether the organizational configuration suits the intended activities. Often, small and medium-sized enterprises experience exponential sales and market share growth but simultaneously need to pay more attention to their organizational structure. In addition, this leads to a point where operations undermine the foundation supporting the entire company framework. Sales volumes increase, and the operational structure struggles to keep up, which tends to deteriorate the company's image in various ways:

- Financial health deteriorates due to inefficient accounts receivable management from credit sales and failure to meet deadlines for tax report submissions. They also need help preparing financial statements and high debt levels to maintain inventory.
- Distribution channels become inefficient due to a need for more resources and personnel to handle customer orders.
- Business operations are neglected because the appropriate areas for addressing the post-sales needs of the customer segment need to be established.

We must ensure our business has the appropriate organizational setup and addresses latent customer needs.

It's also important to acknowledge that management's ambition can weaken the business's position. As a result, this is one of the factors that eventually impacts the company, as efforts are often directed toward capturing new markets and generating higher income, leaving the foundational aspects necessary to support these operations behind. It's essential to consider the following variables:

- ✓ Allocate sufficient time for staff to carry out activities.

- ✓ A sufficient number of skilled employees in different areas will support new operations.
- ✓ Train or select a new sales force to target the new business segment.
- ✓ Evaluate the organization and implement necessary changes to support the new business idea.
- ✓ Strategically establish internal assessments to measure the effectiveness of the business idea.

In the case of a new venture, it's essential to consider the operational structure with which we enter the market, covering three essential points: (1) the cost structure allowing us to be competitive; (2) having the assets (infrastructure, personnel, equipment, and technology) to meet customer demand; and (3) ensuring our sales team can attract the target audience.

If we fail to address these points and still enter the market, we're likely betting on short-term growth. However, this could negatively impact our company's image in the medium term, leading to a loss of market share and potential income.

It's advisable to question whether the business idea is suitable for maximizing income and gaining a larger market share by attracting new customers and retaining existing ones. It's crucial to evaluate the following questions deeply:
- ✓ Does this business idea align with and fulfill current market needs?
- ✓ Is the business idea aligned with our organizational structure? Do we have the capacity to develop it effectively?
- ✓ Will our services bring benefits and add value?

Suppose the answers to these questions are not convincing. In that case, the business idea should be re-evaluated to ensure it produces the expected outcome. However, it's essential to recognize that perfection is unlikely, and all businesses have risks. Our responsibility is to measure the risks we are willing to take, mitigating some of them when possible.

5.1 Feasibility of the Business Idea

We need to assess how feasible it is to implement the new business idea we want to pursue based on conclusions about various aspects involved in business:

- **Technical aspect:** Ensuring we can efficiently provide the proposed service.
- **Financial aspect:** Having the required financial coverage regarding solvency, liquidity, and debt levels when starting a new business idea.
- **Commercial aspect:** Projecting sales in line with market realities and internal expectations.
- **Economic aspect:** Ensuring the business idea generates the expected dividends per shareholders' expectations.
- **Strategic aspect:** Having a strategic position that guarantees market participation and sectoral continuity.

CHAPTER VI: EXECUTION OF THE BUSINESS IDEA

The most critical part of the entire process is execution. While having the best business idea and strategic position is valuable, if we can't execute the business idea, it will remain on paper and in the minds of those who conceived it.

Execution begins with business leaders, those in top management positions. They are responsible for carrying out the execution. If leaders are not committed to the proposed idea, execution won't yield the desired results; we emphasized that the business idea relies on these individuals. They are responsible for executing it and understanding the business's capabilities and the environment in which it operates.

Execution is based on three critical factors:
- It is a discipline and directly related to strategy.
- It is a fundamental activity of senior managers and executives.
- It is the core of the organizational culture.

When we say it's a discipline, we mean that top-level managers and executives must rigorously carry out the strategy daily, following the established frameworks in the business idea to achieve objectives. It's more than just observing how things unfold and requesting reports from subordinates. It involves studying the goal achievement process, getting involved in every task and activity, and asking "what" and "how" questions to ensure fulfillment.

The above involves the following activities:
- ✓ Implementing a rewards system linked to goal achievement.
- ✓ Analyzing the business climate and addressing existing shortcomings to achieve higher employee performance.
- ✓ We are constructing the organizational model for executing the business idea, attracting qualified individuals, and forming a company tailored to the needs.
- ✓ We engage operational areas with the strategy

- ✓ We engage work teams with the business.

When executing a business idea, it's necessary to investigate the current personnel, infrastructure, and operational area. This helps determine whether we have the resources required to fulfill our commitment.

Often, essential resources are not thoroughly considered for a simple reason: key personnel who will execute the idea were not involved. As we've mentioned, if these key individuals are not included, we might have a general idea of our business potential, but only they know our exact capacity.

It's important to note that business ideas are presented to shareholders and investors. Still, they usually differ from the ones designing them. When we are a small business, it's valid to outline the plan with the help of those involved in mid-level decision-making. Relying solely on the owner's perspective is unhealthy, as their view might be clouded by ambition, leading to overvaluation of the business and its resources. That's why having a second opinion is beneficial.

During the execution phase, it's essential to address questions like:
- ✓ What team will be designated to execute the business idea? How will we evaluate them, and how should they account for achieved objectives?
- ✓ What resources do we have for the strategy (technological, structural, financial, human, etc.), and what is needed to carry it out?
- ✓ Will core resources be available within the appropriate timeframe to implement the strategy?
- ✓ Are the objectives achievable within the set timeframe, or do they need to be redesigned to be achieved?
- ✓ Will the strategy itself yield the desired effect on our current business?

Execution should be the core activity of senior managers and executives. If they are not 100% committed to the business, execution will likely be ineffective. They should be deeply involved in execution, controlling all processes required by the business idea. Additionally, they need a clear understanding of operational and personnel processes, including everything from recruitment to staff evaluation.

For instance, in the pen manufacturing factory, if the production plant director is unaware of operational processes and relies solely on reports from the plant manager, they may not find the optimal way to adjust procedures for fulfilling the goals set for their division. This could lead to an incomplete achievement of the strategy's goals due to the director's lack of knowledge.

It's important to understand that activities are delegated, but responsibilities are not. The attainment of general objectives rests on the shoulders of executives, while specific objectives are the responsibility of other collaborators.

In this context, it's never justified for a strategy not to be executed 100% because a middle management employee did not perform their specific task. The ultimate responsibility lies with the executive or manager in charge. It's therefore suggested that executives and managers closely monitor the execution of their subordinates and be ready to provide additional tools or personnel when needed to meet goals.

Creating an organizational culture oriented towards goal execution is valuable for businesses. Implementing the strategic plan won't yield the desired impact if this culture isn't profoundly rooted. Sometimes, the only ones aware of the strategic plan are the business units that are most involved in it. They are traditionally informed about where we are, where we are headed, and how to act to achieve the desired outcomes. Other departments aren't involved, and execution is separate from the company's organizational culture. The result is that the service the business unit aims to provide is compromised because internal departments need to work harmoniously. Each tends to focus on their area as an isolated entity. Essentially, they don't function as a united team.

Finally, executives and managers in charge of business units or teams need to possess essential skills:
   a) Integration with personnel and the business.
   b) Setting realistic goals.
   c) Prioritizing objectives.
   d) Monitoring goals.
   e) Creating a rewards system.
   f) Training staff.
   g) Leveraging individual capabilities.

Next, we explain each of these skills.

6.1 Integration with Personnel and the Business

It's crucial that business leaders know and integrate with their personnel and their business unit. If those with you don't feel close to you, they won't feel comfortable voicing their concerns or presenting their ideas. Ultimately, they will only go the extra mile in their roles if there's a barrier. The primary purpose of those who lead others is to break down all those barriers. Hence, the team feels the support of their leaders and can rely on someone who will advocate for their interests. Getting involved with personnel includes thoroughly understanding each individual, not only in a work context, as our decisions, attitudes, and ways of thinking are influenced by our environment.

We all work in the same business unit and physical space. Still, differences will arise during decision-making because everyone has different backgrounds. For example, they studied elsewhere or have experience in a similar business, making them more knowledgeable about the market. Numerous factors can result in differences in their thinking and approach. Therefore, it's crucial to know each team member beyond their role. This helps assess whom to trust with specific tasks and how that person would react in different situations they might face.

On the other hand, many executives believe they understand their current business. Still, their understanding is often based on experience within the company. Knowing the business doesn't only mean having spent many years in the same company. It involves comprehending the sector in which we operate, its evolution and trends, customer tastes and preferences changes, and other factors affecting the market and our company's internal capabilities. We won't be effective if we only see a snapshot of our business when the reality is different, and customers no longer prefer the same services and products as before. In companies that have been around for over a decade, executives or business owners sometimes believe that consumers still behave the same way as in the beginning and assume that what they did in the past will still work. They insist on continuing the same approach.

By that time, all market participants identified, for example, that they needed to place their products closer to customers and capitalized on the gap to gain more market presence. No matter how much quality we add or how personalized our service becomes, customers will take advantage of the proximity of the stores and stop consuming our products. It's crucial to understand the entire business and not just the current company we are in. We need to look out the window, observe how the market behaves, and analyze how to fix the house to attract more customers.

6.2 Setting Realistic Goals and Prioritizing Objectives

Setting goals requires careful consideration, as incorrectly doing so can have negative consequences. Many executives and business owners set overly demanding goals beyond their company's capabilities, resulting in an undesired reaction among employees. Since these goals are seen as impossible, employees will only make the slightest effort to achieve them.

It's essential to set goals that our employees can fulfill with dedication and effort while being fair and just when making assignments to avoid demotivating the staff. We must be realistic, considering the skills of the personnel, the resources and tools we possess, our market share, our target audience, and the company's structure. Many executives or business owners set goals based on the market share they wish to have and think about their competitors. However, this doesn't align with reality, as competitors likely have different structures, market shares we still need to achieve, more personnel, and the tools to achieve their goals. This not only means setting a goal that has a 60% chance of success but also results in highly demotivated personnel who end up working for the competition.

For example, let's consider that our pen manufacturing factory has a business unit, and the director instructs their team to achieve sales of $180 million by the end of the year. The team consists of three members with the following sales distribution:

1. An executive for urban areas.
2. An executive for the metropolitan area.
3. An executive for large corporations in both urban and metropolitan areas.

The leader has allocated $60 million to each executive to reach the $180 million target by the end of the period. After objecting to the goal, the business unit members have only two options: stay or leave for another company. Assuming all three have survived, the results could be as follows:
1. The urban area executive concluded the period with sales of $7 million.
2. The metropolitan area executive ended the period with sales of $36 million.
3. The large corporation's executive finished the period with sales of $72 million.

Total sales amounted to $115 million, achieving 64% of the budgeted goal due to poor goal distribution. If the director had been more realistic, they would have recognized that urban areas were a very small market for such a demanding sales volume. The executive might have lowered their performance because they would need to come closer to the assigned goal.

On the contrary, the large corporation's executive encountered an easily achievable goal and made only a slight effort, even though they could have achieved more with higher demands. Their market was the largest, but this situation could have led to passive goal attainment. Based on the above, an excessively high goal leads to the same issues as a shallow goal, so we must be careful with our demands to achieve successful execution.

We must set objectives to realize goals and prioritize elements that significantly impact those goals. Transparency is encouraged so employees know where to focus their efforts while keeping sight of other objectives. Suppose we don't prioritize specific tasks and let them process everything according to their criteria. In that case, successful execution might not occur, as higher-impact tasks could be neglected.

6.3 Goal Monitoring

Goal monitoring is a fundamental factor for successful execution. Regular monitoring should be more effective, necessitating the use of a system. Most monitoring occurs through a single channel waiting for a response, but rarely does it involve an appropriate tool for goal achievement.

For instance, if we assign our executives a sales growth target of $60 million by the end of the year, we need to schedule monthly monitoring and measure how goals progress quarterly to verify goal achievement. The focus is not just on measurement but on what we do when the plan isn't being executed as stipulated. It's more than asking how things are going; it's about thinking about how we'll achieve the goals or what's preventing us.

To facilitate execution tools, we present the following scheme:

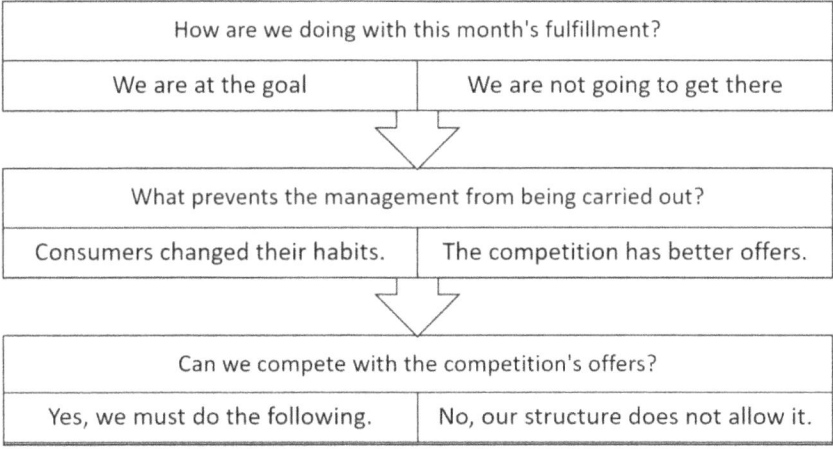

The idea behind this scheme is to stick with the initial plan rather than deeply investigate how progress is being made and what is needed to achieve the goal. Monitoring isn't just about tracking numbers; it goes beyond seeing a black-and-white movie. It's about meeting goals by delving deep enough to identify problems and find alternatives.

6.4 Creating a Rewards Scheme

Developing a rewards scheme based on goal attainment is a highly productive tool for motivating teams to exceed expectations. However, we must be cautious with rewards that are undeserved or unattainable.

A typical case is when a director promotes employees believing they've made significant contributions, are hard workers, have full knowledge of the business, etc. Still, the numbers and management tell a different story. This leads to discontent in various areas, as they understand that no matter how hard they work, they won't be considered for promotions.

Suppose we reward or take on the task of promoting individuals who lack merit. In that case, it will create a sense of discontent within the company among those who have worked hard to fulfill their tasks. Additionally, if the recognition model is based on unattainable goals, this will lead to dissatisfaction among employees as they strive for rewards they won't attain. Similarly, if goals aren't fairly distributed, the reward system won't align with reality, decreasing employee productivity.

Similarly, incentives are granted long after the effort has been made, or else they will have the intended impact. Even if all stirred waters indicate that the tide is for large ships, where admirals send all types of vessels to cross it— even if they sell fishing boats like grand warships— and only a small and humble fishing boat crosses the seas if it reaches land. No one recognizes it upon landing; it will likely face demotivation. That's why providing rewards is essential as soon as goals are achieved.

6.5 Employee Training

It's essential to provide training to our workforce to keep them up-to-date with knowledge and skills that foster the business. It's more costly for our company to hire new personnel than to train those collaborating with us. Developing a career plan for each of our employees is essential so that we have highly skilled personnel as our business grows.

Likewise, training helps us identify potential candidates for promotion in case of employee turnover. Having a backup for each top management and critical position in our business is beneficial to avoid potential temporary disruptions or decreased performance in daily company operations.

6.6 Leveraging Capabilities

A leader who needs to be made aware of their capabilities is destined to remain stagnant. It's crucial that we, as business leaders, understand our strengths and, at the same time, identify those who can assist in areas that are not our forte. However, we must also train ourselves to overcome these weaknesses.

The biggest mistake often made is believing we possess absolute knowledge. The moment this happens, we stop learning and start stagnating. We must be humble enough to recognize that we have much to learn. We need to live like sponges, absorbing the best practices from the market.

CHAPTER VII: BUILD A LEADER FOR EXECUTION

It's essential to be clear that the leader who executes is a valuable piece of the strategic plan, so selecting the right person to take us to the next level must be cautious. The leaders must be authentic in their decisions, a person whom other team members don't influence, and wise or have that "sixth sense" for things to achieve objectives and not just to be well-liked by others.

The person guiding us must know the sector, market, and business, as well as our capabilities and modus operandi. A person who has been successful in another market but needs to gain experience in our market or operate in a completely different realm from our business won't be helpful to us. We need grounded and realistic individuals for execution.

Another quality is self-control in handling situations beyond their control, tolerance, and impartiality, and seeking the best alternatives for the company's benefit. Simultaneously, they must be humble enough to admit they're wrong or have made mistakes.

The profile needs to be developed because we all have opportunities in one of the four aspects mentioned earlier (authenticity, knowledge, self-control, and humility). To handle situations that aren't their strong suit, it is recommended that the right person and a complementary partner be selected, if necessary.

As individuals, we will make mistakes. In such cases, rather than scolding them, it's ideal for guiding, directing, and refocusing them to encourage them to continue performing tasks correctly, thus boosting their self-confidence.
Some of the mistakes that leaders must avoid or underestimate in their management include the following:

- *Underestimating the market and the reality of competitors*. Neglecting other participants in the sector is a widespread mistake among organizational leaders, indicating a deficient sense of urgency. Those who have a perception about the other players are the ones who often react effectively within the industry, meaning that competitors set the pace for the business, and others follow.

- *Not creating highly efficient teams.* Many leaders understand that customers come to their business for the products they sell or the services they provide, overlooking the fact that the people interact. While other competitors form teams, some make the mistake of having insufficient personnel for their tasks, making it difficult for them to react to market changes; this is also a result of leaders needing to focus on motivating members of their organization rather than production or sales growth, as ultimately each member is responsible for driving sales in one way or another.

- *Having a limited organizational vision.* Leaders must develop strategies to achieve the organization's vision. As mentioned, genuine commitment from leaders is needed for the business to function at its maximum capacity.

- *Lack of incentives for goal achievement.* The leader's responsibility is to create rewards for employees who achieve short-term goals, keeping them motivated to fulfill their assignments consistently.

- *Not communicating the organization's vision.* Leaders often keep the organization's planning and vision to themselves. Still, if each employee doesn't know how their work contributes, they won't be able to give the company the total effort it expects. Each member must know the company's vision with certainty to understand the relevance of their work and give it their all.

The leader is responsible for being oriented towards creating and satisfying customers, as they are the driving force behind our business. They are the purpose of everything because if we produce products or provide services, it's for customers to consume them. In business, the followers are the customers, which must be captured by the leader who manages the execution of our action plan.

The organization will only achieve its goals with an influential leader driven by a vibrant will to succeed. There's nothing more motivating than the will to reach where we have set out to go.

In conclusion, a leader's roles go beyond operational improvements, agreement execution, and individual function supervision. Their essence is strategy: defining and communicating the company's unique position and making adjustments between activities. The leader discerns which sector changes and customer the company needs will respond to while also setting the boundaries of the business by determining the target customer group and the needs to address to execute the vision.

FINAL WORDS

For the entire organization, all its members must be aligned with the project's vision and the process of satisfying the target customer rather than focusing on selling the products or services they market. A business starts with the purpose of addressing a specific need, which in turn determines the market niche it's aimed at. A business never begins with the sale or marketing of a particular product, which is one of the major mistakes made by entrepreneurs who introduce products to the market, thinking they are innovative without analyzing how the need this product or service fulfills is being met in the local market. This can lead to a decline in the sales planning they've done.

Customers' needs shape the industry, and it evolves backward, improving the entire process. This means starting with the finished product consumed by customers to study the size and profitability of the market. Suppose profitability is reasonable and costs are covered. In that case, you can step back in the market hierarchy, looking at how to design the product within the local market or importing parts or raw materials. Suppose there's still a market and profitability. In that case, you can move on to producing the raw materials for manufacturing the products. This technique prevents a company from losing focus and remains profitable within the process. This way, the company will maintain its focus because it will be oriented towards the fundamental aspect of providing services to fulfill customer needs rather than focusing on production and product marketing.

Operational effectiveness means performing the same activities better than other competitors. Most ongoing businesses or new entrepreneurs strive to act more efficiently in processes and activities that others already have in their companies. We're not saying this practice is wrong, as improvement is always significant. Still, the point is that if we lack a strategy that sets us apart from others, everything will boil down to who is more efficient in the set of activities. Large corporations have resources that allow them to choose more advanced technologies, pay employees better, and engage in many activities. On the other hand, due to their limited capacities, small businesses need help making operations more efficient. This is why it's necessary to establish a different strategic position compared to other participants.

Strategic positioning involves carrying out different activities from those of other competitors or performing similar activities differently. This positioning is more difficult to imitate because to differentiate from others, you need to determine the company's strategic position and then locate the supporting activities required for that positioning. It functions like a service network that intends to stand out from competitors.

Furthermore, we must always distinguish sales from marketing, although many associate them with similar activities. Each is different, as sales are focused on the needs of the sellers, while marketing is concentrated on the buyers. Sales purely specialize in turning a product into cash (money). In contrast, marketing explores how to satisfy customers' needs through the products or services offered.

A company must understand both aspects clearly; if it only focuses on sales and the production of goods or services for marketing, it will neglect the essence of the business – what the products are meant for and what needs they fulfill in the market. Every business must orient itself towards marketing and create the necessary foundations to encourage buyers to consume the products or services it markets.

Finally, a vital aspect for all entrepreneurs is to initiate the business model with future expansion in mind. The groundwork must be laid to have the execution plan ready when growth demands it. As they mature, many must introduce departments or the right personnel to address expansion needs.

The truth is, improvising as you grow indicates that the business had a demand long ago, and you're merely reacting to a difficulty that has arisen. This is why, over the years, those who didn't foresee the progress they would experience faced challenging situations that cost them the position they achieved. Starting small doesn't mean starting disorganized or without planning.

www.ingramcontent.com/pod-product-compliance
Lightning Source LLC
Chambersburg PA
CBHW050103230526
45470CB00004B/1662